Ben Stacy Jerrik (Ed.)

MidnightBSD

Ben Stacy Jerrik (Ed.)

MidnightBSD

Unix-like, Operating system, FreeBSD

Part Press

Imprint

Permission is granted to copy, distribute and/or modify this document under the terms of the GNU Free Documentation License, Version 1.2 or any later version published by the Free Software Foundation; with no Invariant Sections, with the Front-Cover Texts, and with the Back- Cover Texts. A copy of the license is included in the section entitled "GNU Free Documentation License".

All parts of this book are extracted from Wikipedia, the free encyclopedia (www.wikipedia.org).

You can get detailed informations about the authors of this collection of articles at the end of this book. The editors (Ed.) of this book are no authors. They have not modified or extended the original texts.

Pictures published in this book can be under different licences than the GNU Free Documentation License. You can get detailed informations about the authors and licences of pictures at the end of this book.

The content of this book was generated collaboratively by volunteers. Please be advised that nothing found here has necessarily been reviewed by people with the expertise required to provide you with complete, accurate or reliable information. Some information in this book maybe misleading or wrong. The Publisher does not guarantee the validity of the information found here. If you need specific advice (f.e. in fields of medical, legal, financial, or risk management questions) please contact a professional who is licensed or knowledgeable in that area.

Any brand names and product names mentioned in this book are subject to trademark, brand or patent protection and are trademarks or registered trademarks of their respective holders. The use of brand names, product names, common names, trade names, product descriptions etc. even without a particular marking in this works is in no way to be construed to mean that such names may be regarded as unrestricted in respect of trademark and brand protection legislation and could thus be used by anyone.

Cover image: www.ingimage.com
Concerning the licence of the cover image please contact ingimage.

Publisher:
Part Press is a trademark of
International Book Market Service Ltd., 17 Rue Meldrum, Beau Bassin, 1713-01 Mauritius
Email: info@bookmarketservice.com
Website: www.bookmarketservice.com

Published in 2012

Printed in: U.S.A., U.K., Germany. This book was not produced in Mauritius.

ISBN: 978-613-1-94482-6

Contents

Articles

References

MidnightBSD

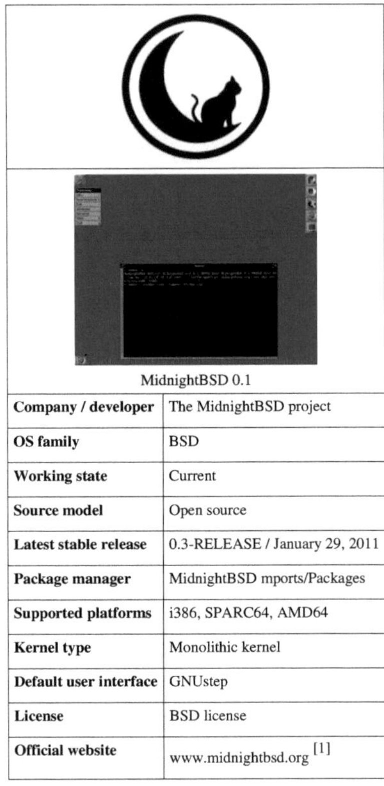

	MidnightBSD 0.1
Company / developer	The MidnightBSD project
OS family	BSD
Working state	Current
Source model	Open source
Latest stable release	0.3-RELEASE / January 29, 2011
Package manager	MidnightBSD mports/Packages
Supported platforms	i386, SPARC64, AMD64
Kernel type	Monolithic kernel
Default user interface	GNUstep
License	BSD license
Official website	www.midnightbsd.org [1]

MidnightBSD is a free Unix-like, desktop-oriented operating system based on FreeBSD 6.1. It borrows heavily from the NEXTSTEP graphical user interface.

History and development

MidnightBSD began as a fork from FreeBSD in 2005. The founder of the project, Lucas Holt, wished to create a BSD derived desktop operating system. He was familiar with several live CD projects, but not the work on PC-BSD or DesktopBSD. At the same time, he also had an interest in GNUstep. The two ideas were folded into a plan to create a user friendly desktop environment. MidnightBSD 0.1 was released based on the efforts of Lucas Holt, Caryn Holt, D. Adam Karim, Phil Pereira of bsdnexus, and Christian Reinhardt. This release features a modified version of the FreeBSD ports system. The ports system evolved into "mports" which includes fake support, generation of packages before installation, license tagging, and strict rules about package list generation and modification of files outside the destination. Many of these features were introduced in MidnightBSD 0.1.1.

Christian Reinhardt replaced Phil Pereira as the lead "mports" maintainer prior to the release of MidnightBSD 0.1. D. Adam Karim acted as the security officer for the first release. All release engineering is handled by Lucas Holt.

0.2 introduced a refined mports system with over 2000 packages. The Portable C Compiler was added on i386 in addition to the GNU Compiler Collection. Other changes include enabling ipfw and sound card detection on startup, newer versions of many software packages including Bind, GCC, OpenSSH, and Sendmail, as well as a Live CD creation system.

Currently, the project is focusing on finishing the Magus build cluster software, creating a new installer, finishing the new package installation and management tools called mport, and beginning work on the 0.3 release. The next release will feature some enhancements found in FreeBSD 7.0 and DragonFly BSD.

Etymology

MidnightBSD is named after Lucas and Caryn Holt's cat, Midnight. Midnight is a ten pound black Turkish Angora.

License

MidnightBSD is released under several licenses. The kernel code and most newly created code is released under the two-clause BSD license. There are parts under the GPL, LGPL, ISC, and Beerware licenses, along with three- and four-clause BSD licenses.

External links

- MidnightBSD Home Page [1]
- MidnightBSD Wiki [2]
- Magus: The MidnightBSD build cluster [3]
- MidnightBSD Developer Blog [4]

References

[1] http://www.midnightbsd.org/
[2] http://www.midnightbsd.org/wiki/
[3] http://www.midnightbsd.org/magus/
[4] http://www.justjournal.com/users/mbsd

Unix-like

A **Unix-like** (sometimes referred to as **UN*X** or ***nix**) operating system is one that behaves in a manner similar to a Unix system, while not necessarily conforming to or being certified to any version of the Single UNIX Specification.

There is no standard for defining the term, and some difference of opinion is possible as to the degree to which a given operating system is "Unix-like".

The term can include free and open source operating systems inspired by Bell Labs' Unix or designed to emulate its features, commercial and proprietary work-alikes, and even versions based on the licensed UNIX source code (which may be sufficiently "Unix-like" to pass certification and bear the "UNIX" trademark).

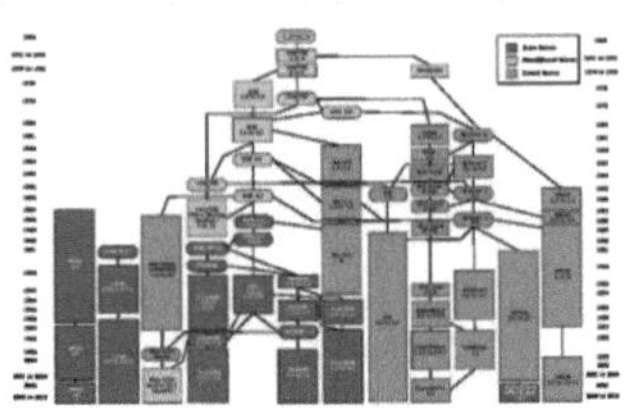
Diagram of the relationships between the major Unix-like systems

Definition

The Open Group owns the UNIX trademark and administers the Single UNIX Specification, with the "UNIX" name being used as a certification mark. They do not approve of the construction "Unix-like", and consider it a misuse of their trademark. Their guidelines require "UNIX" to be presented in uppercase or otherwise distinguished from the surrounding text, strongly encourage using it as a branding adjective for a generic word such as "system", and discourage its use in hyphenated phrases.[1]

Other parties frequently treat "Unix" as a genericized trademark. Some add a wildcard character to the name to make an abbreviation like "Un*x"[2] or "*nix", since Unix-like systems often have Unix-like names such as AIX, HP-UX, IRIX, Linux, Minix, Ultrix, and Xenix. These patterns do not literally match many system names, but are still generally recognized to refer to any UNIX descendant or work-alike system, even those with completely dissimilar names such as Solaris or FreeBSD.

In 2007, Wayne R. Gray sued to dispute the status of UNIX as a trademark, but lost his case, and lost again on appeal.

Also in 2007, the Open Group reached a binding legal agreement to prevent the German University of Kassel from using "UNIK" as its short form name.[3]

History

"Unix-like" systems started to appear in the late 1970s and early 1980s. Many proprietary versions, such as Idris (1978), UNOS (1982), Coherent (1983), and UniFlex (1985), aimed to provide businesses with the functionality available to academic users of UNIX.

When AT&T later allowed commercial licensing of UNIX in the 1980s, a variety of proprietary systems were developed based on it, including AIX, HP-UX, IRIX, SunOS, Tru64, Ultrix, and Xenix. These largely displaced the proprietary clones. Growing incompatibility between these systems led to the creation of interoperability standards, including POSIX and the Single UNIX Specification.

Meanwhile, the GNU Project was launched in 1983 with the goal of making GNU, an operating system which all computer users could freely use, study, modify, and redistribute. Various "Unix-like" operating systems developed alongside GNU, frequently sharing substantial components with it (leading to some disagreement about whether they should be called "GNU" or not). These primarily served as low-cost and unrestricted substitutes for UNIX, and include 4.4BSD, Linux, and Minix. Some of these have in turn been the basis for commercial "Unix-like" systems, such as BSD/OS and Mac OS X. Notably, Mac OS X 10.5 and Mac OS X 10.6 running on Intel Macs are certified under the Single UNIX Specification.[4]

The various BSD variants are notable in that they are in fact descendants of UNIX, developed by the University of California at Berkeley with UNIX source code from Bell Labs. However, the BSD code base has evolved since then, replacing all of the AT&T code. Since the BSD variants are not certified as compliant with the Single UNIX Specification (except for Mac OS X 10.5 Leopard and Mac OS X 10.6 Snow Leopard), they are referred to as "UNIX-like".

Categories

Dennis Ritchie, one of the original creators of Unix, has expressed his opinion that Unix-like systems such as Linux are *de facto* Unix systems.[5] Eric S. Raymond and Rob Langley have suggested[6] that there are three kinds of Unix-like systems:

Genetic UNIX

> Those systems with a historical connection to the AT&T codebase. Most (but not all) commercial UNIX systems fall into this category. So do the BSD systems, which are descendants of work done at the University of California, Berkeley in the late 1970s and early 1980s. Some of these systems have no original AT&T code but can still trace their ancestry to AT&T designs.

Trademark or Branded UNIX

> These systems—largely commercial in nature—have been determined by the Open Group to meet the Single UNIX Specification and are allowed to carry the UNIX name. Most such systems are commercial derivatives of the System V code base in one form or another, although Apple Mac OS X 10.5 and later is a BSD variant, and has been certified, and a few certified systems (such as IBM z/OS) earned the trademark through a POSIX compatibility layer and are not otherwise inherently Unix systems. Many ancient UNIX systems no longer meet this definition.

Functional UNIX

> Broadly, any Unix-like system that behaves in a manner roughly consistent with the UNIX specification; more specifically, this can refer to systems such as Linux or Minix that behave similarly to a UNIX system but have no genetic or trademark connection to the AT&T code base. Most free/open-source implementations of the UNIX design, whether genetic UNIX or not, fall into the restricted definition of this third category due to the expense of obtaining Open Group certification, which costs thousands of dollars, not being commercially necessary.

Compatibility layers

Some non-Unix-like operating systems provide a Unix-like compatibility layer, with variable degrees of Unix-like functionality.

- IBM z/OS's UNIX System Services is sufficiently complete to be certified as trademark UNIX.
- Cygwin and MSYS both provide a reasonably complete GNU environment, sufficient for most common open source software to be compiled and run, with some emulation of Linux, on top of the Microsoft Windows user API.
- Interix provides Unix-like functionality as a Windows NT subsystem.

See also

- Berkeley Software Distribution
- Linux distribution
- List of Linux distributions
- List of Unix utilities
- List of operating systems

References

[1] Trademark Guidelines (http://www.opengroup.org/tm-guidelines.htm) The Open Group.
[2] Eric S. Raymond; Guy L. Steele Jr.. "UN*X" (http://catb.org/jargon/html/U/UN-asterisk-X.html). *The Jargon File.* . Retrieved 2009-01-22.
[3] Publik, Kasseler Hochschulzeitung (http://www.uni-kassel.de/presse/publik/07_03/s1.pdf) Nummer 3, 17 April 2007
[4] Register of Open Branded Products (http://www.opengroup.org/openbrand/register/) The Open Group
[5] Interview with Dennis M. Ritchie (http://www.linuxfocus.org/English/July1999/article79.html) Manuel Benet, *LinuxFocus*, July 1999
[6] The meaning of 'Unix' (http://catb.org/~esr/hackerlore/sco-vs-ibm.html#id305450) Eric Raymond and Rob Langley, *OSI Position Paper on the SCO-vs.-IBM Complaint*

External links

- Unix-like Definition (http://www.linfo.org/unix-like.html) by The Linux Information Project (LINFO)
- UNIX history (http://www.levenez.com/unix/) a history time line graph of most UNIX and Unix-like systems by Éric Lévénez
- Grokline's UNIX Ownership History Project (http://grokline.net/) a project to map out the technical history of UNIX and Unix-like systems

Operating_system

An **operating system (OS)** is a set of software that manages computer hardware resources and provides common services for computer programs. The operating system is a vital component of the system software in a computer system. Application programs require an operating system to function.

Time-sharing operating systems schedule tasks for efficient use of the system and may also include accounting for cost allocation of processor time, mass storage, printing, and other resources.

For hardware functions such as input and output and memory allocation, the operating system acts as an intermediary between programs and the computer hardware,[1] [2] although the application code is usually executed directly by the hardware and will frequently make a system call to an OS function or be interrupted by it. Operating systems can be found on almost any device that contains a computer—from cellular phones and video game consoles to supercomputers and web servers.

Examples of popular modern operating systems include Android, BSD, iOS, GNU/Linux, Mac OS X, Microsoft Windows,[3] Windows Phone, and IBM z/OS. All these, except Windows and z/OS, share roots in UNIX.

Types

Real-time

A real-time operating system is a multitasking operating system that aims at executing real-time applications. Real-time operating systems often use specialized scheduling algorithms so that they can achieve a deterministic nature of behavior. The main objective of real-time operating systems is their quick and predictable response to events. They have an event-driven or time-sharing design and often aspects of both. An event-driven system switches between tasks based on their priorities or external events while time-sharing operating systems switch tasks based on clock interrupts.

Multi-user

A multi-user operating system allows multiple users to access a computer system concurrently. Time-sharing system can be classified as multi-user systems as they enable a multiple user access to a computer through the sharing of time. Single-user operating systems, as opposed to a multi-user operating system, are usable by a single user at a time. Being able to use multiple accounts on a Windows operating system does not make it a multi-user system. Rather, only the network administrator is the real user. But for a UNIX-like operating system, it is possible for two users to login at a time and this capability of the OS makes it a multi-user operating system.

Multi-tasking vs. Single-tasking

When only a single program is allowed to run at a time, the system is grouped under a single-tasking system. However, when the operating system allows the execution of multiple tasks at one time, it is classified as a multi-tasking operating system. Multi-tasking can be of two types: pre-emptive or co-operative. In pre-emptive multitasking, the operating system slices the CPU time and dedicates one slot to each of the programs. Unix-like operating systems such as Solaris and Linux support pre-emptive multitasking, as does AmigaOS. Cooperative multitasking is achieved by relying on each process to give time to the other processes in a defined manner. 16-bit versions of Microsoft Windows used cooperative multi-tasking. 32-bit versions, both Windows NT and Win9x, used pre-emptive multi-tasking. Mac OS prior to OS X used to support cooperative multitasking.

Distributed

Further information: Distributed system

A distributed operating system manages a group of independent computers and makes them appear to be a single computer. The development of networked computers that could be linked and communicate with each other gave rise to distributed computing. Distributed computations are carried out on more than one machine. When computers in a group work in cooperation, they make a distributed system.

Embedded

Embedded operating systems are designed to be used in embedded computer systems. They are designed to operate on small machines like PDAs with less autonomy. They are able to operate with a limited number of resources. They are very compact and extremely efficient by design. Windows CE and Minix 3 are some examples of embedded operating systems.

Summary

Early computers were built to perform a series of single tasks, like a calculator. Operating systems did not exist in their modern and more complex forms until the early 1960s.[4] Basic operating system features were developed in the 1950s, such as resident monitor functions that could automatically run different programs in succession to speed up processing. Hardware features were added that enabled use of runtime libraries, interrupts, and parallel processing. When personal computers by companies such as Apple Inc., Atari, IBM and Amiga became popular in the 1980s, vendors included operating systems in them that had previously become widely used on mainframe and mini computers.

History

In the 1940s, the earliest electronic digital systems had no operating systems. Electronic systems of this time were so primitive compared to those of today that instructions were often entered into the system one bit at a time on rows of mechanical switches or by jumper wires on plug boards. These were special-purpose systems that, for example, generated ballistics tables for the military or controlled the printing of payroll checks from data on punched paper cards. After programmable general purpose computers were invented, machine languages (consisting of strings of the binary digits 0 and 1 on punched paper tape) were introduced that sped up the programming process (Stern, 1981).

In the early 1950s, a computer could execute only one program at a time. Each user had sole use of the computer for a limited period of time and would arrive at a scheduled time with program and data on punched paper cards and/or punched tape. The program would be loaded into the machine, and the machine would be set to work until the program completed or crashed. Programs could generally be debugged via a front panel using toggle switches and panel lights. It is said that Alan Turing was a master of this on the early Manchester Mark 1 machine, and he was already deriving the primitive conception of an operating system from the principles of the Universal Turing machine.[4]

Later machines came with libraries of programs, which would be linked to a user's program to assist in operations such as input and output and generating computer code from human-readable symbolic code. This was the genesis of the modern-day computer system. However, machines still ran a single job at a time. At Cambridge University in England the job queue was at one time a washing line from which tapes were hung with different colored clothes-pegs to indicate job-priority.

OS/360 was used on most IBM mainframe computers beginning in 1966, including the computers that helped NASA put a man on the moon.

Mainframes

Through the 1950s, many major features were pioneered in the field of operating systems, including batch processing, input/output interrupt, buffering, multitasking, spooling, runtime libraries, link-loading, and programs for sorting records in files. These features were included or not included in application software at the option of application programmers, rather than in a separate operating system used by all applications. In 1959 the SHARE Operating System was released as an integrated utility for the IBM 704, and later in the 709 and 7090 mainframes, although it was quickly supplanted by IBSYS/IBJOB on the 709, 7090 and 7094.

During the 1960s, IBM's OS/360 introduced the concept of a single OS spanning an entire product line, which was crucial for the success of the System/360 machines. IBM's current mainframe operating systems are distant descendants of this original system and applications written for OS/360 can still be run on modern machines.

OS/360 also pioneered the concept that the operating system keeps track of all of the system resources that are used, including program and data space allocation in main memory and file space in secondary storage, and file locking during update. When the process is terminated for any reason, all of these resources are re-claimed by the operating system.

The alternative CP-67 system for the S/360-67 started a whole line of IBM operating systems focused on the concept of virtual machines. Other operating systems used on IBM S/360 series mainframes included systems developed by IBM: COS/360 (Compatibility Operating System), DOS/360 (Disk Operating System), TSS/360 (Time Sharing System), TOS/360 (Tape Operating System), BOS/360 (Basic Operating System), and ACP (Airline Control Program), as well as a few non-IBM systems: MTS (Michigan Terminal System), MUSIC (Multi-User System for Interactive Computing), and ORVYL (Stanford Timesharing System).

Control Data Corporation developed the SCOPE operating system in the 1960s, for batch processing. In cooperation with the University of Minnesota, the Kronos and later the NOS operating systems were developed during the 1970s, which supported simultaneous batch and timesharing use. Like many commercial timesharing systems, its interface was an extension of the Dartmouth BASIC operating systems, one of the pioneering efforts in timesharing and programming languages. In the late 1970s, Control Data and the University of Illinois developed the PLATO operating system, which used plasma panel displays and long-distance time sharing networks. Plato was remarkably innovative for its time, featuring real-time chat, and multi-user graphical games. Burroughs Corporation introduced the B5000 in 1961 with the MCP, (Master Control Program) operating system. The B5000 was a stack machine designed to exclusively support high-level languages with no machine language or assembler, and indeed the MCP was the first OS to be written exclusively in a high-level language – ESPOL, a dialect of ALGOL. MCP also introduced many other ground-breaking innovations, such as being the first commercial implementation of virtual memory. During development of the AS400, IBM made an approach to Burroughs to licence MCP to run on the AS400 hardware. This proposal was declined by Burroughs management to protect its existing hardware production. MCP is still in use today in the Unisys ClearPath/MCP line of computers.

UNIVAC, the first commercial computer manufacturer, produced a series of EXEC operating systems. Like all early main-frame systems, this was a batch-oriented system that managed magnetic drums, disks, card readers and line printers. In the 1970s, UNIVAC produced the Real-Time Basic (RTB) system to support large-scale time sharing, also patterned after the Dartmouth BC system.

General Electric and MIT developed General Electric Comprehensive Operating Supervisor (GECOS), which introduced the concept of ringed security privilege levels. After acquisition by Honeywell it was renamed to General Comprehensive Operating System (GCOS).

Digital Equipment Corporation developed many operating systems for its various computer lines, including TOPS-10 and TOPS-20 time sharing systems for the 36-bit PDP-10 class systems. Prior to the widespread use of UNIX, TOPS-10 was a particularly popular system in universities, and in the early ARPANET community.

In the late 1960s through the late 1970s, several hardware capabilities evolved that allowed similar or ported software to run on more than one system. Early systems had utilized microprogramming to implement features on their systems in order to permit different underlying computer architectures to appear to be the same as others in a series. In fact most 360s after the 360/40 (except the 360/165 and 360/168) were microprogrammed implementations. But soon other means of achieving application compatibility were proven to be more significant.

The enormous investment in software for these systems made since 1960s caused most of the original computer manufacturers to continue to develop compatible operating systems along with the hardware. The notable supported mainframe operating systems include:

- Burroughs MCP – B5000, 1961 to Unisys Clearpath/MCP, present.
- IBM OS/360 – IBM System/360, 1966 to IBM z/OS, present.
- IBM CP-67 – IBM System/360, 1967 to IBM z/VM, present.
- UNIVAC EXEC 8 – UNIVAC 1108, 1967, to OS 2200 Unisys Clearpath Dorado, present.

Microcomputers

The first microcomputers did not have the capacity or need for the elaborate operating systems that had been developed for mainframes and minis; minimalistic operating systems were developed, often loaded from ROM and known as *monitors*. One notable early disk operating system was CP/M, which was supported on many early microcomputers and was closely imitated by Microsoft's MS-DOS, which became wildly popular as the operating system chosen for the IBM PC (IBM's version of it was called IBM DOS or PC DOS). In the '80s, Apple Computer Inc. (now Apple Inc.) abandoned its popular Apple II series of microcomputers to introduce the Apple Macintosh computer with an innovative Graphical User Interface (GUI) to the Mac OS.

The introduction of the Intel 80386 CPU chip with 32-bit architecture and paging capabilities, provided personal computers with the ability to run multitasking operating systems like those of earlier minicomputers and mainframes. Microsoft responded to this progress by hiring Dave Cutler, who had developed the VMS operating system for Digital Equipment Corporation. He would lead the development of the Windows NT operating system, which continues to serve as the basis for Microsoft's operating systems line. Steve Jobs, a co-founder of Apple Inc., started NeXT Computer Inc., which developed the Unix-like NEXTSTEP operating system. NEXTSTEP would later be acquired by Apple Inc. and used, along with code from FreeBSD as the core of Mac OS X.

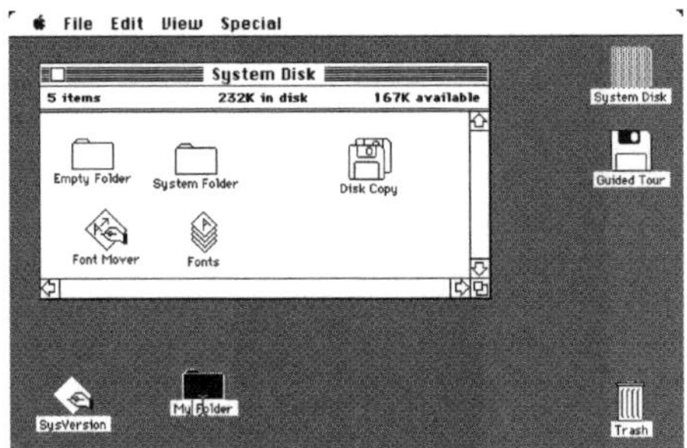

PC-DOS was an early personal computer OS that featured a command line interface.

Mac OS by Apple Computer became the first widespread OS to feature a graphical user interface. Many of its features such as windows and icons would later become commonplace in GUIs.

The GNU Project was started by activist and programmer Richard Stallman with the goal of a complete free software replacement to the proprietary UNIX operating system. While the project was highly successful in duplicating the functionality of various parts of UNIX, development of the GNU Hurd kernel proved to be unproductive. In 1991, Finnish computer science student Linus Torvalds, with cooperation from volunteers collaborating over the Internet, released the first version of the Linux kernel. It was soon merged with the GNU user space components and system software to form a complete operating system. Since then, the combination of the two major components has usually been referred to as simply "Linux" by the software industry, a naming convention that Stallman and the Free Software Foundation remain opposed to, preferring the name GNU/Linux. The Berkeley Software Distribution, known as BSD, is the UNIX derivative distributed by the University of California, Berkeley, starting in the 1970s. Freely distributed and ported to many minicomputers, it eventually also gained a following for use on PCs, mainly as FreeBSD, NetBSD and OpenBSD.

Examples of operating systems

UNIX and UNIX-like operating systems

Ken Thompson wrote B, mainly based on BCPL, which he used to write Unix, based on his experience in the MULTICS project. B was replaced by C, and Unix developed into a large, complex family of inter-related operating systems which have been influential in every modern operating system (see History).

The *UNIX-like* family is a diverse group of operating systems, with several major sub-categories including System V, BSD, and GNU/Linux. The name "UNIX" is a trademark of The Open Group which licenses it for use with any operating system that has been shown to conform to their definitions. "UNIX-like" is commonly used to refer to the large set of operating systems which resemble the original UNIX.

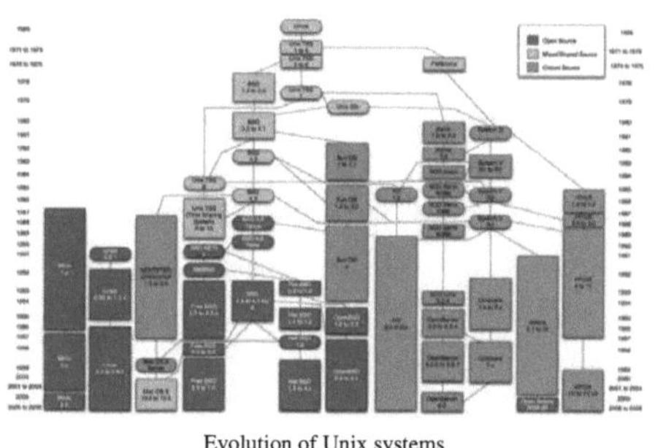
Evolution of Unix systems

Unix-like systems run on a wide variety of computer architectures. They are used heavily for servers in business, as well as workstations in academic and engineering environments. Free UNIX variants, such as GNU/Linux and BSD, are popular in these areas.

Four operating systems are certified by the The Open Group (holder of the Unix trademark) as Unix. HP's HP-UX and IBM's AIX are both descendants of the original System V Unix and are designed to run only on their respective vendor's hardware. In contrast, Sun Microsystems's Solaris Operating System can run on multiple types of hardware, including x86 and Sparc servers, and PCs. Apple's Mac OS X, a replacement for Apple's earlier (non-Unix) Mac OS, is a hybrid kernel-based BSD variant derived from NeXTSTEP, Mach, and FreeBSD.

Unix interoperability was sought by establishing the POSIX standard. The POSIX standard can be applied to any operating system, although it was originally created for various Unix variants.

BSD and its descendants

A subgroup of the Unix family is the Berkeley Software Distribution family, which includes FreeBSD, NetBSD, and OpenBSD, PC-BSD. These operating systems are most commonly found on webservers, although they can also function as a personal computer OS. The Internet owes much of its existence to BSD, as many of the protocols now commonly used by computers to connect, send and receive data over a network were widely implemented and refined in BSD. The world wide web was also first demonstrated on a number of computers running an OS based on BSD called NextStep.

BSD has its roots in Unix. In 1974, University of California, Berkeley installed its first Unix system.

The first server for the World Wide Web ran on NeXTSTEP, based on BSD.

Over time, students and staff in the computer science department there began adding new programs to make things easier, such as text editors. When Berkely received new VAX computers in 1978 with Unix installed, the school's undergraduates modified Unix even more in order to take advantage of the computer's hardware possibilities. The Defense Advanced Research Projects Agency of the US Department of Defense took interest, and decided to fund the project. Many schools, corporations, and government organizations took notice and started to use Berkeley's version of Unix instead of the official one distributed by AT&T.

Steve Jobs, upon leaving Apple Inc. in 1985, formed NeXT Inc., a company that manufactured high-end computers running on a variation of BSD called NeXTSTEP. One of these computers was used by Tim Berners-Lee as the first webserver to create the World Wide Web.

Developers like Keith Bostic encouraged the project to replace any non-free code that originated with Bell Labs. Once this was done, however, AT&T sued. Eventually, after two years of legal disputes, the BSD project came out ahead and spawned a number of free derivatives, such as FreeBSD and NetBSD.

Mac OS X

Mac OS X is a line of open core graphical operating systems developed, marketed, and sold by Apple Inc., the latest of which is pre-loaded on all currently shipping Macintosh computers. Mac OS X is the successor to the original Mac OS, which had been Apple's primary operating system since 1984. Unlike its predecessor, Mac OS X is a UNIX operating system built on technology that had been developed at NeXT through the second half of the 1980s and up until Apple purchased the company in early 1997.

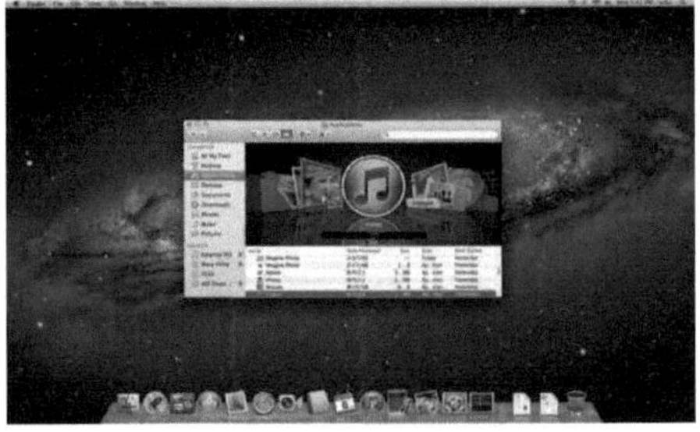

The standard user interface of Mac OS X

The operating system was first released in 1999 as Mac OS X Server 1.0, with a desktop-oriented version (Mac OS X v10.0 "Cheetah") following in March 2001. Since then, six more distinct "client" and "server" editions of Mac OS X have been released, the most recent being OS X 10.8 "Mountain Lion", which was first made available on February 16, 2012 for developers, and to be released to the public late summer 2012. Releases of Mac OS X are named after big cats.

The server edition, Mac OS X Server, is architecturally identical to its desktop counterpart but usually runs on Apple's line of Macintosh server hardware. Mac OS X Server includes work group management and administration software tools that provide simplified access to key network services, including a mail transfer agent, a Samba server, an LDAP server, a domain name server, and others. In Mac OS X v10.7 Lion, all server aspects of Mac OS X Server have been integrated into the client version.[5]

Linux and GNU

Linux (or GNU/Linux) is a Unix-like operating system that was developed without any actual Unix code, unlike BSD and its variants. Linux can be used on a wide range of devices from supercomputers to wristwatches. The Linux kernel is released under an open source license, so anyone can read and modify its code. It has been modified to run on a large variety of electronics. Although estimates suggest that Linux is used on 1.82% of all personal computers,[6] [7] it has been widely adopted for use in servers[8] and embedded systems[9] (such as cell phones). Linux has superseded Unix in most places, and is used on the 10 most powerful supercomputers in the world.[10] The Linux kernel is used in some popular distributions, such as Red Hat, Debian, Ubuntu, Linux Mint and Google's Android.

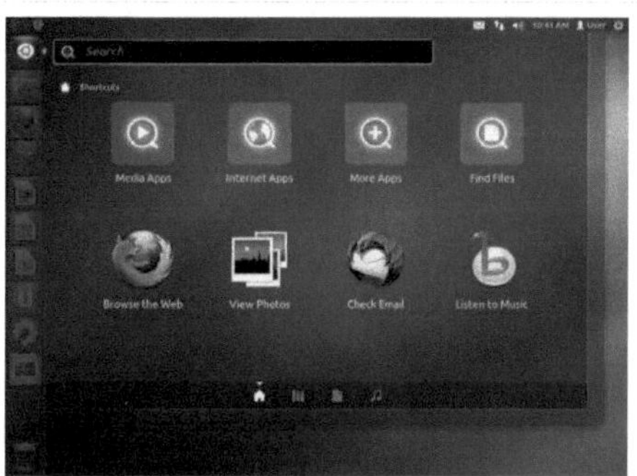

Ubuntu, desktop Linux distribution

The GNU project is a mass collaboration of programmers who seek to create a completely free and open operating system that was similar to Unix but with completely original code. It was started in 1983 by Richard Stallman, and is responsible for many of the parts of most Linux variants. Thousands of pieces of software for virtually every operating system are licensed under the GNU General Public License. Meanwhile, the Linux kernel began as a side project of Linus Torvalds, a university student from Finland. In 1991, Torvalds began work on it, and posted information about his project on a newsgroup for computer students and programmers. He received a wave of support and volunteers who ended up creating a full-fledged kernel. Programmers from GNU took notice, and members of both projects worked to integrate the finished GNU parts with the Linux kernel in order to create a full-fledged operating system.

Android, a popular mobile operating system
using the Linux kernel

Google Chrome OS

Chrome is an operating system based on the Linux kernel and designed by Google. Since Chrome OS targets computer users who spend most of their time on the Internet, it is mainly a web browser with no ability to run applications. It relies on Internet applications (or Web apps) used in the web browser to accomplish tasks such as word processing and media viewing, as well as online storage for storing most files.

Microsoft Windows

Microsoft Windows is a family of proprietary operating systems designed by Microsoft Corporation and primarily targeted to Intel architecture based computers, with an estimated 88.9 percent total usage share on Web connected computers.[7] [11] [12] [13] The newest version is Windows 7 for workstations and Windows Server 2008 R2 for servers. Windows 7 recently overtook Windows XP as most used OS.[14] [15] [16]

Bootable Windows To Go USB flash drive

Microsoft Windows originated in 1985 as an application running on top of MS-DOS, which was the standard operating system shipped on most Intel architecture personal computers at the time. In 1995, Windows 95 was released which only used MS-DOS as a bootstrap. For backwards compatibility, Win9x could run real-mode MS-DOS[17] [18] and 16 bits Windows 3.x[19] drivers. Windows Me, released in 2000, was the last version in the Win9x family. Later versions have all been based on the Windows NT kernel. Current versions of Windows run on IA-32 and x86-64 microprocessors, although Windows 8 will support ARM architecture. In the past, Windows NT supported non-Intel architectures.

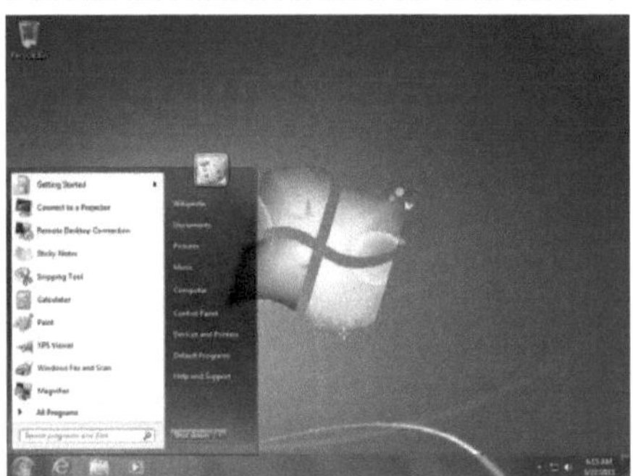
Microsoft Windows 7 Desktop

Server editions of Windows are widely used. In recent years, Microsoft has expended significant capital in an effort to promote the use of Windows as a server operating environment. However, Windows' usage on servers is not as widespread as on personal computers, as Windows competes against Linux and BSD for server market share.[20] [21]

Other

There have been many operating systems that were significant in their day but are no longer so, such as AmigaOS; OS/2 from IBM and Microsoft; Mac OS, the non-Unix precursor to Apple's Mac OS X; BeOS; XTS-300; RISC OS; MorphOS and FreeMint. Some are still used in niche markets and continue to be developed as minority platforms for enthusiast communities and specialist applications. OpenVMS formerly from DEC, is still under active development by Hewlett-Packard. Yet other operating systems are used almost exclusively in academia, for operating systems education or to do research on operating system concepts. A typical example of a system that fulfills both roles is MINIX, while for example Singularity is used purely for research.

Other operating systems have failed to win significant market share, but have introduced innovations that have influenced mainstream operating systems, not least Bell Labs' Plan 9.

Components

The components of an operating system all exist in order to make the different parts of a computer work together. All software—from financial databases to film editors—needs to go through the operating system in order to use any of the hardware, whether it be as simple as a mouse or keyboard or complex as an Internet connection.

Kernel

With the aid of the firmware and device drivers, the kernel provides the most basic level of control over all of the computer's hardware devices. It manages memory access for programs in the RAM, it determines which programs get access to which hardware resources, it sets up or resets the CPU's operating states for optimal operation at all times, and it organizes the data for long-term non-volatile storage with file systems on such media as disks, tapes, flash memory, etc.

Applications

Kernel

CPU   Memory   Devices

A kernel connects the application software to the hardware of a computer.

Program execution

The operating system provides an interface between an application program and the computer hardware, so that an application program can interact with the hardware only by obeying rules and procedures programmed into the operating system. The operating system is also a set of services which simplify development and execution of application programs. Executing an application program involves the creation of a process by the operating system kernel which assigns memory space and other resources, establishes a priority for the process in multi-tasking systems, loads program binary code into memory, and initiates execution of the application program which then interacts with the user and with hardware devices.

Interrupts

Interrupts are central to operating systems, as they provide an efficient way for the operating system to interact with and react to its environment. The alternative — having the operating system "watch" the various sources of input for events (polling) that require action — can be found in older systems with very small stacks (50 or 60 bytes) but are unusual in modern systems with large stacks. Interrupt-based programming is directly supported by most modern CPUs. Interrupts provide a computer with a way of automatically saving local register contexts, and running specific code in response to events. Even very basic computers support hardware interrupts, and allow the programmer to specify code which may be run when that event takes place.

When an interrupt is received, the computer's hardware automatically suspends whatever program is currently running, saves its status, and runs computer code previously associated with the interrupt; this is analogous to placing a bookmark in a book in response to a phone call. In modern operating systems, interrupts are handled by the operating system's kernel. Interrupts may come from either the computer's hardware or from the running program.

When a hardware device triggers an interrupt, the operating system's kernel decides how to deal with this event, generally by running some processing code. The amount of code being run depends on the priority of the interrupt (for example: a person usually responds to a smoke detector alarm before answering the phone). The processing of hardware interrupts is a task that is usually delegated to software called device driver, which may be either part of the operating system's kernel, part of another program, or both. Device drivers may then relay information to a running program by various means.

A program may also trigger an interrupt to the operating system. If a program wishes to access hardware for example, it may interrupt the operating system's kernel, which causes control to be passed back to the kernel. The kernel will then process the request. If a program wishes additional resources (or wishes to shed resources) such as memory, it will trigger an interrupt to get the kernel's attention.

Modes

Modern CPUs support multiple modes of operation. CPUs with this capability use at least two modes: protected mode and supervisor mode. The supervisor mode is used by the operating system's kernel for low level tasks that need unrestricted access to hardware, such as controlling how memory is written and erased, and communication with devices like graphics cards. Protected mode, in contrast, is used for almost everything else. Applications operate within protected mode, and can only use hardware by communicating with the kernel, which controls everything in supervisor mode. CPUs might have other modes similar to protected mode as well,

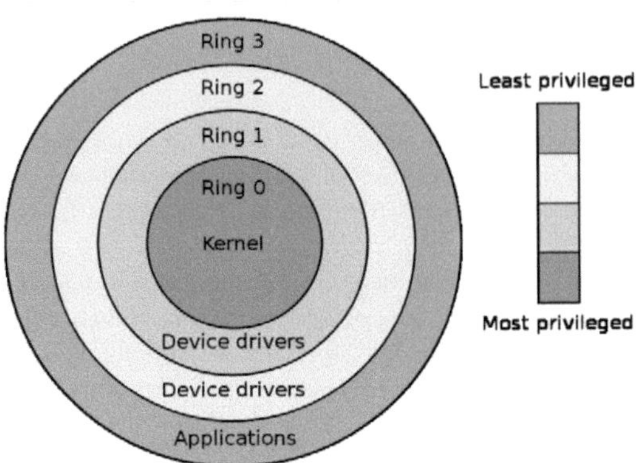

Privilege rings for the x86 available in protected mode. Operating systems determine which processes run in each mode.

such as the virtual modes in order to emulate older processor types, such as 16-bit processors on a 32-bit one, or 32-bit processors on a 64-bit one.

When a computer first starts up, it is automatically running in supervisor mode. The first few programs to run on the computer, being the BIOS or EFI, bootloader, and the operating system have unlimited access to hardware - and this is required because, by definition, initializing a protected environment can only be done outside of one. However, when the operating system passes control to another program, it can place the CPU into protected mode.

In protected mode, programs may have access to a more limited set of the CPU's instructions. A user program may leave protected mode only by triggering an interrupt, causing control to be passed back to the kernel. In this way the operating system can maintain exclusive control over things like access to hardware and memory.

The term "protected mode resource" generally refers to one or more CPU registers, which contain information that the running program isn't allowed to alter. Attempts to alter these resources generally causes a switch to supervisor mode, where the operating system can deal with the illegal operation the program was attempting (for example, by killing the program).

Memory management

Among other things, a multiprogramming operating system kernel must be responsible for managing all system memory which is currently in use by programs. This ensures that a program does not interfere with memory already in use by another program. Since programs time share, each program must have independent access to memory.

Cooperative memory management, used by many early operating systems, assumes that all programs make voluntary use of the kernel's memory manager, and do not exceed their allocated memory. This system of memory management is almost never seen any more, since programs often contain bugs which can cause them to exceed their allocated memory. If a program fails, it may cause memory used by one or more other programs to be affected or overwritten. Malicious programs or viruses may purposefully alter another program's memory, or may affect the operation of the operating system itself. With cooperative memory management, it takes only one misbehaved program to crash the system.

Memory protection enables the kernel to limit a process' access to the computer's memory. Various methods of memory protection exist, including memory segmentation and paging. All methods require some level of hardware support (such as the 80286 MMU), which doesn't exist in all computers.

In both segmentation and paging, certain protected mode registers specify to the CPU what memory address it should allow a running program to access. Attempts to access other addresses will trigger an interrupt which will cause the CPU to re-enter supervisor mode, placing the kernel in charge. This is called a segmentation violation or Seg-V for short, and since it is both difficult to assign a meaningful result to such an operation, and because it is usually a sign of a misbehaving program, the kernel will generally resort to terminating the offending program, and will report the error.

Windows 3.1-Me had some level of memory protection, but programs could easily circumvent the need to use it. A general protection fault would be produced, indicating a segmentation violation had occurred; however, the system would often crash anyway.

Virtual memory

Further information: Page fault

The use of virtual memory addressing (such as paging or segmentation) means that the kernel can choose what memory each program may use at any given time, allowing the operating system to use the same memory locations for multiple tasks.

If a program tries to access memory that isn't in its current range of accessible memory, but nonetheless has been allocated to it, the kernel will be interrupted in the same way as it would if the program were to exceed its allocated memory. (See section on memory management.) Under UNIX this kind of interrupt is referred to as a page fault.

When the kernel detects a page fault it will generally adjust the virtual memory range of the program which triggered it, granting it access to the memory requested. This gives the kernel discretionary power over where a particular application's memory is stored, or even whether or not it has actually been allocated yet.

In modern operating systems, memory which is accessed less frequently can be temporarily stored on disk or other media to make that space available for use by other programs. This is called swapping, as an area of memory can be used by multiple programs, and what that memory area contains can be swapped or exchanged on demand.

"Virtual memory" provides the programmer or the user with the perception that there is a much larger amount of RAM in the computer than is really there.[22]

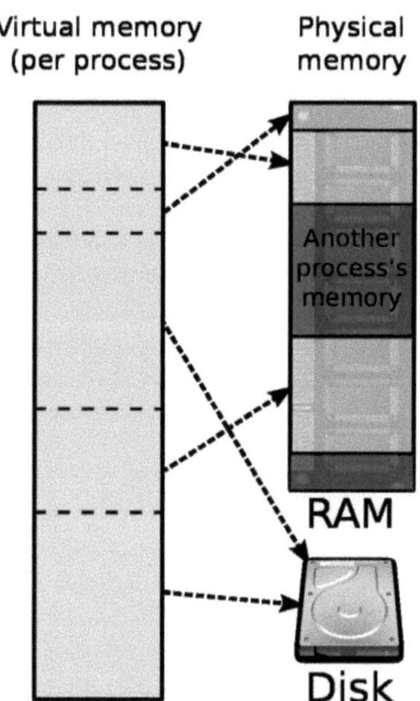

Many operating systems can "trick" programs into using memory scattered around the hard disk and RAM as if it is one continuous chunk of memory, called virtual memory.

Multitasking

Further information: Context switch, Preemptive multitasking, and Cooperative multitasking

Multitasking refers to the running of multiple independent computer programs on the same computer; giving the appearance that it is performing the tasks at the same time. Since most computers can do at most one or two things at one time, this is generally done via time-sharing, which means that each program uses a share of the computer's time to execute.

An operating system kernel contains a piece of software called a scheduler which determines how much time each program will spend executing, and in which order execution control should be passed to programs. Control is passed to a process by the kernel, which allows the program access to the CPU and memory. Later, control is returned to the kernel through some mechanism, so that another program may be allowed to use the CPU. This so-called passing of control between the kernel and applications is called a context switch.

An early model which governed the allocation of time to programs was called cooperative multitasking. In this model, when control is passed to a program by the kernel, it may execute for as long as it wants before explicitly returning control to the kernel. This means that a malicious or malfunctioning program may not only prevent any other programs from using the CPU, but it can hang the entire system if it enters an infinite loop.

Modern operating systems extend the concepts of application preemption to device drivers and kernel code, so that the operating system has preemptive control over internal run-times as well.

The philosophy governing preemptive multitasking is that of ensuring that all programs are given regular time on the CPU. This implies that all programs must be limited in how much time they are allowed to spend on the CPU without being interrupted. To accomplish this, modern operating system kernels make use of a timed interrupt. A protected mode timer is set by the kernel which triggers a return to supervisor mode after the specified time has elapsed. (See above sections on Interrupts and Dual Mode Operation.)

On many single user operating systems cooperative multitasking is perfectly adequate, as home computers generally run a small number of well tested programs. The AmigaOS is an exception, having pre-emptive multitasking from its very first version. Windows NT was the first version of Microsoft Windows which enforced preemptive multitasking, but it didn't reach the home user market until Windows XP (since Windows NT was targeted at professionals).

Disk access and file systems

Access to data stored on disks is a central feature of all operating systems. Computers store data on disks using files, which are structured in specific ways in order to allow for faster access, higher reliability, and to make better use out of the drive's available space. The specific way in which files are stored on a disk is called a file system, and enables files to have names and attributes. It also allows them to be stored in a hierarchy of directories or folders arranged in a directory tree.

Early operating systems generally supported a single type of disk drive and only one kind of file system. Early file systems were limited in their capacity, speed, and in the kinds of file names and directory

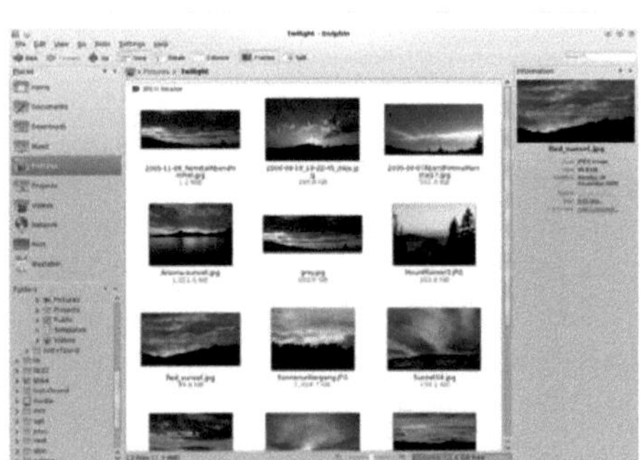

Filesystems allow users and programs to organize and sort files on a computer, often through the use of directories (or "folders")

structures they could use. These limitations often reflected limitations in the operating systems they were designed for, making it very difficult for an operating system to support more than one file system.

While many simpler operating systems support a limited range of options for accessing storage systems, operating systems like UNIX and GNU/Linux support a technology known as a virtual file system or VFS. An operating system such as UNIX supports a wide array of storage devices, regardless of their design or file systems, allowing them to be accessed through a common application programming interface (API). This makes it unnecessary for programs to have any knowledge about the device they are accessing. A VFS allows the operating system to provide programs with access to an unlimited number of devices with an infinite variety of file systems installed on them, through the use of specific device drivers and file system drivers.

A connected storage device, such as a hard drive, is accessed through a device driver. The device driver understands the specific language of the drive and is able to translate that language into a standard language used by the operating system to access all disk drives. On UNIX, this is the language of block devices.

When the kernel has an appropriate device driver in place, it can then access the contents of the disk drive in raw format, which may contain one or more file systems. A file system driver is used to translate the commands used to access each specific file system into a standard set of commands that the operating system can use to talk to all file systems. Programs can then deal with these file systems on the basis of filenames, and directories/folders, contained within a hierarchical structure. They can create, delete, open, and close files, as well as gather various information about them, including access permissions, size, free space, and creation and modification dates.

Various differences between file systems make supporting all file systems difficult. Allowed characters in file names, case sensitivity, and the presence of various kinds of file attributes makes the implementation of a single interface for every file system a daunting task. Operating systems tend to recommend using (and so support natively) file systems specifically designed for them; for example, NTFS in Windows and ext3 and ReiserFS in GNU/Linux. However, in practice, third party drives are usually available to give support for the most widely used file systems in most general-purpose operating systems (for example, NTFS is available in GNU/Linux through NTFS-3g, and ext2/3 and ReiserFS are available in Windows through FS-driver [23] and rfstool [24]).

Support for file systems is highly varied among modern operating systems, although there are several common file systems which almost all operating systems include support and drivers for. Operating systems vary on file system support and on the disk formats they may be installed on. Under Windows, each file system is usually limited in application to certain media; for example, CDs must use ISO 9660 or UDF, and as of Windows Vista, NTFS is the only file system which the operating system can be installed on. It is possible to install GNU/Linux onto many types of file systems. Unlike other operating systems, GNU/Linux and UNIX allow any file system to be used regardless of the media it is stored in, whether it is a hard drive, a disc (CD,DVD...), a USB flash drive, or even contained within a file located on another file system.

Device drivers

A device driver is a specific type of computer software developed to allow interaction with hardware devices. Typically this constitutes an interface for communicating with the device, through the specific computer bus or communications subsystem that the hardware is connected to, providing commands to and/or receiving data from the device, and on the other end, the requisite interfaces to the operating system and software applications. It is a specialized hardware-dependent computer program which is also operating system specific that enables another program, typically an operating system or applications software package or computer program running under the operating system kernel, to interact transparently with a hardware device, and usually provides the requisite interrupt handling necessary for any necessary asynchronous time-dependent hardware interfacing needs.

The key design goal of device drivers is abstraction. Every model of hardware (even within the same class of device) is different. Newer models also are released by manufacturers that provide more reliable or better performance and these newer models are often controlled differently. Computers and their operating systems cannot be expected to know how to control every device, both now and in the future. To solve this problem, operating systems essentially dictate how every type of device should be controlled. The function of the device driver is then to translate these operating system mandated function calls into device specific calls. In theory a new device, which is controlled in a new manner, should function correctly if a suitable driver is available. This new driver will ensure that the device appears to operate as usual from the operating system's point of view.

Under versions of Windows before Vista and versions of Linux before 2.6, all driver execution was co-operative, meaning that if a driver entered an infinite loop it would freeze the system. More recent revisions of these operating systems incorporate kernel preemption, where the kernel interrupts the driver to give it tasks, and then separates itself from the process until it receives a response from the device driver, or gives it more tasks to do.

Networking

Currently most operating systems support a variety of networking protocols, hardware, and applications for using them. This means that computers running dissimilar operating systems can participate in a common network for sharing resources such as computing, files, printers, and scanners using either wired or wireless connections. Networks can essentially allow a computer's operating system to access the resources of a remote computer to support the same functions as it could if those resources were connected directly to the local computer. This includes everything from simple communication, to using networked file systems or even sharing another computer's graphics or sound hardware. Some network services allow the resources of a computer to be accessed transparently, such as SSH which allows networked users direct access to a computer's command line interface.

Client/server networking allows a program on a computer, called a client, to connect via a network to another computer, called a server. Servers offer (or host) various services to other network computers and users. These services are usually provided through ports or numbered access points beyond the server's network address. Each port number is usually associated with a maximum of one running program, which is responsible for handling requests to that port. A daemon, being a user program, can in turn access the local hardware resources of that computer by passing requests to the operating system kernel.

Many operating systems support one or more vendor-specific or open networking protocols as well, for example, SNA on IBM systems, DECnet on systems from Digital Equipment Corporation, and Microsoft-specific protocols (SMB) on Windows. Specific protocols for specific tasks may also be supported such as NFS for file access. Protocols like ESound, or esd can be easily extended over the network to provide sound from local applications, on a remote system's sound hardware.

Security

A computer being secure depends on a number of technologies working properly. A modern operating system provides access to a number of resources, which are available to software running on the system, and to external devices like networks via the kernel.

The operating system must be capable of distinguishing between requests which should be allowed to be processed, and others which should not be processed. While some systems may simply distinguish between "privileged" and "non-privileged", systems commonly have a form of requester *identity*, such as a user name. To establish identity there may be a process of *authentication*. Often a username must be quoted, and each username may have a password. Other methods of authentication, such as magnetic cards or biometric data, might be used instead. In some cases, especially connections from the network, resources may be accessed with no authentication at all (such as reading files over a network share). Also covered by the concept of requester **identity** is *authorization*; the particular services and resources accessible by the requester once logged into a system are tied to either the requester's user account or to the variously configured groups of users to which the requester belongs.

In addition to the allow/disallow model of security, a system with a high level of security will also offer auditing options. These would allow tracking of requests for access to resources (such as, "who has been reading this file?"). Internal security, or security from an already running program is only possible if all possibly harmful requests must be carried out through interrupts to the operating system kernel. If programs can directly access hardware and resources, they cannot be secured.

External security involves a request from outside the computer, such as a login at a connected console or some kind of network connection. External requests are often passed through device drivers to the operating system's kernel, where they can be passed onto applications, or carried out directly. Security of operating systems has long been a concern because of highly sensitive data held on computers, both of a commercial and military nature. The United States Government Department of Defense (DoD) created the *Trusted Computer System Evaluation Criteria* (TCSEC) which is a standard that sets basic requirements for assessing the effectiveness of security. This became of vital importance to operating system makers, because the TCSEC was used to evaluate, classify and select trusted operating systems being considered for the processing, storage and retrieval of sensitive or classified information.

Network services include offerings such as file sharing, print services, email, web sites, and file transfer protocols (FTP), most of which can have compromised security. At the front line of security are hardware devices known as firewalls or intrusion detection/prevention systems. At the operating system level, there are a number of software firewalls available, as well as intrusion detection/prevention systems. Most modern operating systems include a software firewall, which is enabled by default. A software firewall can be configured to allow or deny network traffic to or from a service or application running on the operating system. Therefore, one can install and be running an insecure service, such as Telnet or FTP, and not have to be threatened by a security breach because the firewall would deny all traffic trying to connect to the service on that port.

An alternative strategy, and the only sandbox strategy available in systems that do not meet the Popek and Goldberg virtualization requirements, is the operating system not running user programs as native code, but instead either emulates a processor or provides a host for a p-code based system such as Java.

Internal security is especially relevant for multi-user systems; it allows each user of the system to have private files that the other users cannot tamper with or read. Internal security is also vital if auditing is to be of any use, since a program can potentially bypass the operating system, inclusive of bypassing auditing.

User interface

Every computer that is to be operated by an individual requires a user interface. The user interface is not actually a part of the operating system—it generally runs in a separate program usually referred to as a shell, but is essential if human interaction is to be supported. The user interface requests services from the operating system that will acquire data from input hardware devices, such as a keyboard, mouse or credit card reader, and requests operating system services to display prompts, status messages and such on output hardware devices, such as a video monitor or printer. The two most common forms of a user interface have historically been the command-line interface, where computer commands are typed out line-by-line, and the graphical user interface, where a visual environment (most commonly a WIMP) is present.

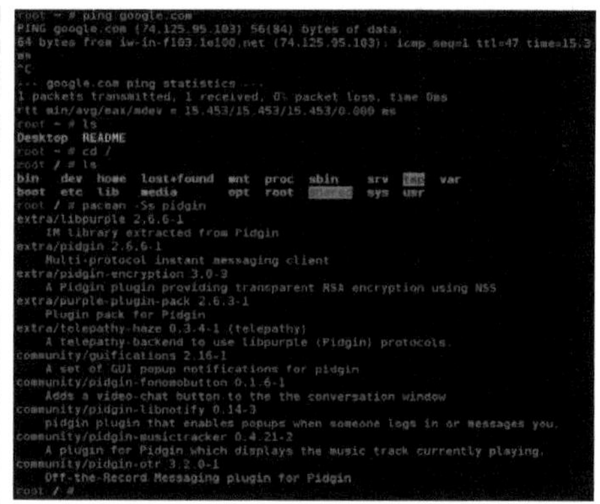

A screenshot of the Bourne Again Shell command line. Each command is typed out after the 'prompt', and then its output appears below, working its way down the screen. The current command prompt is at the bottom.

Graphical user interfaces

A screenshot of the KDE graphical user interface. Programs take the form of images on the screen, and the files, folders (directories), and applications take the form of icons and symbols. A mouse is used to navigate the computer.

Most of the modern computer systems support graphical user interfaces (GUI), and often include them. In some computer systems, such as the original implementation of Mac OS, the GUI is integrated into the kernel.

While technically a graphical user interface is not an operating system service, incorporating support for one into the operating system kernel can allow the GUI to be more responsive by reducing the number of context switches required for the GUI to perform its output functions. Other operating systems are modular, separating the graphics subsystem from the kernel and the Operating System. In the 1980s UNIX, VMS and many others had operating systems that were built this way. GNU/Linux and Mac OS X are also built this way. Modern releases of Microsoft Windows such as Windows Vista implement a graphics subsystem that is mostly in user-space; however the graphics drawing routines of versions between Windows NT 4.0 and Windows Server 2003 exist mostly in kernel space. Windows 9x had very little distinction between the interface and the kernel.

Many computer operating systems allow the user to install or create any user interface they desire. The X Window System in conjunction with GNOME or KDE is a commonly found setup on most Unix and Unix-like (BSD, GNU/Linux, Solaris) systems. A number of Windows shell replacements have been released for Microsoft Windows, which offer alternatives to the included Windows shell, but the shell itself cannot be separated from Windows.

Numerous Unix-based GUIs have existed over time, most derived from X11. Competition among the various vendors of Unix (HP, IBM, Sun) led to much fragmentation, though an effort to standardize in the 1990s to COSE and CDE failed for various reasons, and were eventually eclipsed by the widespread adoption of GNOME and KDE. Prior to free software-based toolkits and desktop environments, Motif was the prevalent toolkit/desktop combination (and was the basis upon which CDE was developed).

Graphical user interfaces evolve over time. For example, Windows has modified its user interface almost every time a new major version of Windows is released, and the Mac OS GUI changed dramatically with the introduction of Mac OS X in 1999.[25]

Real-time operating systems

A real-time operating system (RTOS) is a multitasking operating system intended for applications with fixed deadlines (real-time computing). Such applications include some small embedded systems, automobile engine controllers, industrial robots, spacecraft, industrial control, and some large-scale computing systems.

An early example of a large-scale real-time operating system was Transaction Processing Facility developed by American Airlines and IBM for the Sabre Airline Reservations System.

Embedded systems that have fixed deadlines use a real-time operating system such as VxWorks, PikeOS, eCos, QNX, MontaVista Linux and RTLinux. Windows CE is a real-time operating system that shares similar APIs to desktop Windows but shares none of desktop Windows' codebase. Symbian OS also has an RTOS kernel (EKA2) starting with version 8.0b.

Some embedded systems use operating systems such as Palm OS, BSD, and GNU/Linux, although such operating systems do not support real-time computing.

Operating system development as a hobby

Operating system development is one of the most complicated activities in which a computing hobbyist may engage. A hobby operating system may be classified as one whose code has not been directly derived from an existing operating system, and has few users and active developers. [26]

In some cases, hobby development is in support of a "homebrew" computing device, for example, a simple single-board computer powered by a 6502 microprocessor. Or, development may be for an architecture already in widespread use. Operating system development may come from entirely new concepts, or may commence by modeling an existing operating system. In either case, the hobbyist is his/her own developer, or may interact with a small and sometimes unstructured group of individuals who have like interests.

Examples of a hobby operating system include ReactOS and Syllable.

Diversity of operating systems and portability

Application software is generally written for use on a specific operating system, and sometimes even for specific hardware. When porting the application to run on another OS, the functionality required by that application may be implemented differently by that OS (the names of functions, meaning of arguments, etc.) requiring the application to be adapted, changed, or otherwise maintained.

This cost in supporting operating systems diversity can be avoided by instead writing applications against software platforms like Java, or Qt for web browsers. These abstractions have already borne the cost of adaptation to specific operating systems and their system libraries.

Another approach is for operating system vendors to adopt standards. For example, POSIX and OS abstraction layers provide commonalities that reduce porting costs.

See also

- Comparison of operating systems
- Handheld computers
- Hypervisor
- Interruptible operating system
- List of important publications in operating systems
- List of operating systems
- Microcontroller

- Network operating system
- Object-oriented operating system
- Operating System Projects
- PCjacking
- System image
- Timeline of operating systems
- Usage share of operating systems

References

[1] Stallings (2005). *Operating Systems, Internals and Design Principles*. Pearson: Prentice Hall. p. 6.

[2] Dhotre, I.A. (2009). *Operating Systems.*. Technical Publications. p. 1.

[3] "Operating System Market Share" (http://marketshare.hitslink.com/operating-system-market-share.aspx?qprid=10). Net Applications. .

[4] Hansen, Per Brinch, ed. (2001). *Classic Operating Systems* (http://books.google.com/?id=-PDPBvIPYBkC&lpg=PP1& pg=PP1#v=onepage&q). Springer. pp. 4–7. ISBN 0-387-95113-X. .

[5] http://www.apple.com/macosx/lion/

[6] Usage share of operating systems

[7] "Top 5 Operating Systems from January to April 2011" (http://gs.statcounter.com/#os-ww-monthly-201101-201104-bar). StatCounter. October 2009. . Retrieved November 5, 2009.

[8] IDC report into Server market share (http://www.idc.com/about/viewpressrelease.jsp?containerId=prUS22360110§ionId=null& elementId=null&pageType=SYNOPSIS)

[9] GNU/Linux still top embedded OS (http://www.linuxdevices.com/news/NS4920597981.html)

[10] TOP500 List – November 2010 (1–100) | TOP500 Supercomputing Sites (http://www.top500.org/list/2010/11/100)

[11] "Global Web Stats" (http://marketshare.hitslink.com/operating-system-market-share.aspx?qprid=8). Net Market Share, Net Applications. May 2011. . Retrieved 2011-05-07.

[12] "Global Web Stats" (http://www.w3counter.com/globalstats.php). W3Counter, Awio Web Services. September 2009. . Retrieved
      2009-10-24.
[13] "Operating System Market Share" (http://marketshare.hitslink.com/operating-system-market-share.aspx?qprid=8). Net Applications.
      October 2009. . Retrieved November 5, 2009.
[14] "w3schools.com OS Platform Statistics" (http://www.w3schools.com/browsers/browsers_os.asp). . Retrieved October 30, 2011.
[15] "Stats Count Global Stats Top Five Operating Systems" (http://gs.statcounter.com/#os-ww-monthly-201010-201110). . Retrieved
      October 30, 2011.
[16] "Global statistics at w3counter.com" (http://www.w3counter.com/globalstats.php). . Retrieved 23 January 2012.
[17] http://support.microsoft.com/kb/130179/EN-US
[18] http://support.microsoft.com/kb/134748/en
[19] http://support.microsoft.com/kb/163354/en
[20] "Operating System Share by Groups for Sites in All Locations January 2009" (http://news.netcraft.com/SSL-Survey/CMatch/osdv_all). .
[21] "Behind the IDC data: Windows still No. 1 in server operating systems" (http://blogs.zdnet.com/microsoft/?p=5408). ZDNet.
      2010-02-26. .
[22] Stallings, William (2008). *Computer Organization & Architecture*. New Delhi: Prentice-Hall of India Private Limited. p. 267.
      ISBN 978-81-203-2962-1.
[23] http://www.fs-driver.org
[24] http://p-nand-q.com/download/rfstool.html
[25] Poisson, Ken. "Chronology of Personal Computer Software" (http://www.islandnet.com/~kpolsson/compsoft/soft1998.htm). Retrieved
      on 2008-05-07. Last checked on 2009-03-30.
[26] "My OS is less hobby than yours" (http://www.osnews.com/story/22638/My_OS_Is_Less_Hobby_than_Yours). *Osnews*. December 21,
      2009. . Retrieved December 21, 2009.

Further reading

- Auslander, Marc A.; Larkin, David C.; Scherr, Allan L. (1981). *The evolution of the MVS Operating System* (http://www.research.ibm.com/journal/rd/255/auslander.pdf). IBM J. Research & Development.
- Deitel, Harvey M.; Deitel, Paul; Choffnes, David. *Operating Systems*. Pearson/Prentice Hall. ISBN 978-0-13-092641-8.
- Bic, Lubomur F.; Shaw, Alan C. (2003). *Operating Systems*. Pearson: Prentice Hall.
- Silberschatz, Avi; Galvin, Peter; Gagne, Greg (2008). *Operating Systems Concepts*. John Wiley & Sons. ISBN 0-470-12872-0.

External links

- Operating Systems (http://www.dmoz.org/Computers/Software/Operating_Systems/) at the Open Directory Project
- Multics History (http://www.cbi.umn.edu/iterations/haigh.html) and the history of operating systems
- How Stuff Works - Operating Systems (http://computer.howstuffworks.com/operating-system.htm)
- Help finding your Operating System type and version (http://whatsmyos.com)

FreeBSD

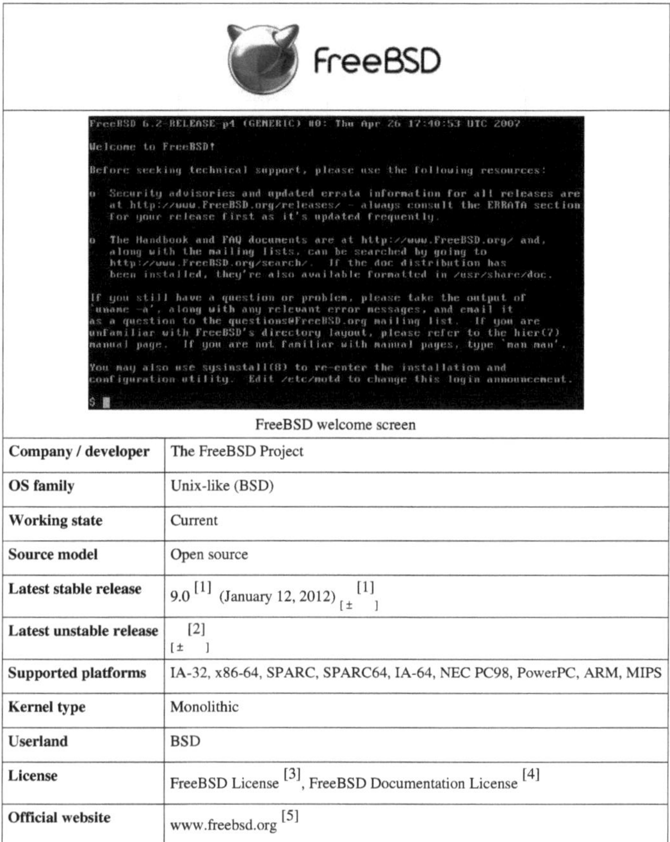

FreeBSD welcome screen

Company / developer	The FreeBSD Project
OS family	Unix-like (BSD)
Working state	Current
Source model	Open source
Latest stable release	9.0 [1] (January 12, 2012) [± [1]]
Latest unstable release	[2] [±]
Supported platforms	IA-32, x86-64, SPARC, SPARC64, IA-64, NEC PC98, PowerPC, ARM, MIPS
Kernel type	Monolithic
Userland	BSD
License	FreeBSD License [3], FreeBSD Documentation License [4]
Official website	www.freebsd.org [5]

FreeBSD is a free Unix-like operating system descended from AT&T UNIX via BSD UNIX. Although for legal reasons FreeBSD cannot be called "UNIX",[6] as the direct descendant of BSD UNIX (many of whose original developers became FreeBSD developers), FreeBSD's internals and system APIs are UNIX-compliant. Thanks to its permissive licensing terms, much of FreeBSD's code base has become an integral part of other operating systems such as OS X that have subsequently been certified as UNIX-compliant and have formally received UNIX branding.[7] With the exception of the proprietary OS X, FreeBSD is the most widely used BSD-derived operating system in terms of number of installed computers, and is the most widely used freely licensed, open-source BSD distribution, accounting for more than three-quarters of all installed systems running free, open-source BSD derivatives.[8]

FreeBSD is a complete operating system. The kernel, device drivers, and all of the userland utilities, such as the shell, are held in the same source code revision tracking tree.[9] (This is in contrast to Linux distributions, for which the kernel, userland utilities, and applications are developed separately, and then packaged together in various ways by others.) Third-party application software may be installed using various software installation systems, the two most common being source installation and package installation, both of which use the FreeBSD Ports system.

FreeBSD was characterised in 2005 as "the unknown giant among free operating systems"[10] and is regarded as reliable and robust.[11]

History

FreeBSD development began in 1993 with a quickly growing, unofficial *patchkit* maintained by users of the 386BSD operating system. This patchkit forked from 386BSD and grew into an operating system taken from U.C. Berkeley's 4.3BSD-Lite (Net/2) tape with many 386BSD components and code from the Free Software Foundation. After two public beta releases via FTP (1.0-GAMMA on September 2, 1993, and 1.0-EPSILON on October 3, 1993), the first official release was FreeBSD 1.0, available via FTP on November 1, 1993 and on CDROM on December 30, 1993. This official release was coordinated by Jordan Hubbard, Nate Williams and Rodney W. Grimes with the name thought up by David Greenman. Walnut Creek CDROM agreed to distribute FreeBSD on CD and gave the project a machine to work on along with a fast Internet connection, which Hubbard later said helped stir FreeBSD's rapid growth. A "highly successful" FreeBSD 1.1 release followed in May 1994.[12]

However, there were legal concerns about the BSD Net/2 release source code used in 386BSD. After a lawsuit between UNIX copyright owner at the time Unix System Laboratories and the University of California, Berkeley, the FreeBSD project re-engineered most of the system using the 4.4BSD-Lite release from Berkeley, which, owing to this lawsuit, had none of the AT&T source code earlier BSD versions had depended upon, making it an unbootable operating system. Following much work, the unencumbered outcome was released as FreeBSD 2.0 in January 1995.[12]

FreeBSD 2.0 featured a revamp of the original Carnegie Mellon University Mach virtual memory system, which was optimized for performance under high loads. This release also introduced the FreeBSD Ports system, which made downloading, building and installing third party software very easy. By 1996 FreeBSD had become popular among commercial and ISP users, powering extremely successful sites like Walnut Creek CD-ROM (a huge repository of software that broke several throughput records on the Internet), Yahoo! and Hotmail. The last release along the 2-STABLE branch was 2.2.8 in November 1998.[13] FreeBSD 3.0 brought many more changes, including the switch to the ELF binary format. Support for SMP systems and the 64-bit Alpha platform were also added. The 3-STABLE branch ended with 3.5.1 in June 2000.[12]

Features

Networking

FreeBSD's TCP/IP stack is based on the 4.2BSD implementation of TCP/IP which greatly contributed to the widespread adoption of these protocols.[14] FreeBSD also supports IPv6, SCTP, IPSec, IPX, AppleTalk and wireless networking.

Storage

FreeBSD has several unique features related to storage. Soft updates maintain filesystem integrity in the event of a system crash. The GEOM framework provides features such as RAID (levels 0, 1, 3 currently), full disk encryption, and concatenation of drives. Filesystem snapshots allow an image of a filesystem at an instant in time to be efficiently created. Snapshots allow reliable backup of a live filesystem. FreeBSD also provides the ZFS filesystem as an alternative to the normal UFS2 file system.

Security

FreeBSD provides several security-related features including access control lists (ACLs), security event auditing, extended file system attributes, fine-grained capabilities and mandatory access controls (MAC). These security enhancements were developed by the **TrustedBSD** project. The project was founded by Robert Watson with the goal of implementing concepts from the Common Criteria for Information Technology Security Evaluation and the Orange Book. This project is ongoing and many of its extensions have been integrated into FreeBSD.

The project has also ported the NSA's FLASK/TE implementation from SELinux to FreeBSD. Other work includes the development of OpenBSM, an open source implementation of Sun's Basic Security Module (BSM) API and audit log file format, which supports an extensive security audit system. This was shipped as part of FreeBSD 6.2. Other infrastructure work in FreeBSD performed as part of the TrustedBSD Project has included SYN cookies, GEOM and OpenPAM.

While most components of the TrustedBSD project are eventually folded into the main sources for FreeBSD, many features, once fully matured, find their way into other operating systems. For example, OpenPAM and UFS2 have been adopted by NetBSD. Moreover, the TrustedBSD MAC Framework has been adopted by Apple for OS X.

Much of this work was sponsored by DARPA.

Portability

FreeBSD has been ported to a variety of processor architectures. The FreeBSD project organizes architectures into tiers that characterize the level of support provided. Tier 1 architectures are mature and fully supported. Tier 2 architectures are undergoing major development. Tier 3 architectures are experimental or are no longer under active development (as is the case of DEC Alpha) and tier 4 architectures have no support at all.

FreeBSD has been ported to the following architectures:[15]

Architecture	Support Level	Notes
x86 (IA-32)	Tier 1	referred to as "i386"
x86-64	Tier 1	referred to as "amd64"
NEC PC-9801	Tier 2	referred to as "pc98"
Sun SPARC	Tier 2	Only support 64-bit (V9) architecture
Itanium (IA-64)	Tier 2	
PowerPC and PowerPC/64	Tier 2	
ARM	Tier 2	
MIPS	Tier 3	
Microsoft's Xbox	Tier 3	
DEC Alpha	Tier 3	Support discontinued from FreeBSD 7.0 on

Third-party software

FreeBSD has a repository of thousands of applications that are developed by third parties outside of the project itself. (Examples include windowing systems, Internet browsers, email programs, office suites, and so forth.) In general, the project itself does not develop this software, only the framework to allow these programs to be installed (termed the *Ports Collection*). Applications may be installed either from source, if its licensing terms allow such redistribution (these are called *ports*), or as compiled binaries if allowed (these are called *packages*). The *Ports Collection* supports the latest release on the -*CURRENT* and -*STABLE* branches. Older releases are not supported and may or may not work correctly with an up-to-date ports collection.[16]

FreeBSD running GIMP, Firefox, and GNOME installed from the ports collection.

Ports Collection

Each application in the *Ports Collection* is installed from source. Each port's Makefile automatically fetches the application source code, either from a local disk, CD-ROM or via ftp, unpacks it on the system, applies the patches, and compiles. This method can be very time consuming as compiling large packages can take hours, but the user is able to install a customized program.[17]

Packages system

For most ports, precompiled binary packages also exist. This method is very quick as the whole compilation process is avoided, but the user is not able to install a program with customized compile time options.[18]

Utilities for managing ports and packages

There are many utilities available for managing ports and packages available in GUIs and CLIs. These are some of them:[19]

- portmaster - A CLI frontend to the ports system, which itself has no dependencies to other ports.[20]
- portupgrade - Another older CLI frontend to the ports system.[21]
- portaudit - A tool to check if versions of installed ports are listed as being vulnerable to security issues.
- barry - A KDE frontend to the ports system
- bpm - A GUI ports collection manager
- kports - A KDE frontend to the ports system
- pib - A GUI Ports Collection management tool

Linux compatibility

Most software that runs on Linux can run on FreeBSD without the need for any compatibility layer. FreeBSD nonetheless still provides a compatibility layer for several other Unix-like operating systems, including Linux. Hence, most Linux binaries can be run on FreeBSD, including some proprietary applications distributed only in binary form. Examples of applications that can use the Linux compatibility layer are StarOffice, the Linux version of Firefox, Adobe Acrobat, RealPlayer, Oracle, Mathematica, Maple, MATLAB, WordPerfect, Skype, Wolfenstein: Enemy Territory, Doom 3 and Quake 4 [22] (though some of these applications also have a native version). No noticeable performance penalty over native FreeBSD programs has been noted when running Linux binaries, and, in some cases, these may even perform more smoothly than on Linux.[23] However, the layer is not altogether seamless, and some Linux binaries are unusable or only partially usable on FreeBSD. This is often because the compatibility layer only supports system calls available in the historical Linux kernel 2.4.2. There is support for Linux 2.6.16 system calls, available since FreeBSD 7.0 and enabled by default since FreeBSD 8.0. However, there is currently no support for running 64-bit Linux binaries.[24]

Development

As of March 2010 FreeBSD had more than 400 active developers[25] and thousands of contributors.

Governance structure

The FreeBSD Project is run by FreeBSD committers, or developers who have CVS/SVN commit access. There are several kinds of committers, including source committers (base operating system), doc committers (documentation and web site authors) and ports (third party application porting and infrastructure). Every two years the FreeBSD committers select a 9-member FreeBSD Core Team who are responsible for overall project direction, setting and enforcing project rules and approving new "commit bits", or the granting of CVS/SVN commit access. A number of responsibilities are officially assigned to other development teams by the FreeBSD Core Team, including responsibility for security advisories (the Security Officer Team), release engineering (the Release Engineering Team) and managing the ports collection (the Port Manager team). Developers may give up their commit rights to retire or for "safe-keeping" after a period of a year or more of inactivity, although commit rights will generally be restored on request. Under rare circumstances commit rights may be removed by Core Team vote as a result of repeated violation of project rules and standards. The FreeBSD Project is unusual among open source projects in having developers who have worked with its source base for over 25 years, owing to the involvement of a number of past University of California developers who worked on BSD at the Computer Systems Research Group.[26]

Branches

FreeBSD developers maintain at least two branches of simultaneous development. The *-CURRENT* branch always represents the "bleeding edge" of FreeBSD development. A *-STABLE* branch of FreeBSD is created for each major version number, from which -RELEASE are cut about once every 4–6 months. If a feature is sufficiently stable and mature it will likely be backported (*MFC* or *Merge from CURRENT* in FreeBSD developer slang) to the *-STABLE* branch.[27] FreeBSD's development model is further described in an article by Niklas Saers.[28]

Foundation

FreeBSD development is supported in part by the FreeBSD Foundation. The foundation is a non-profit organization that accepts donations to fund FreeBSD development. Such funding has been used to sponsor developers for specific activities, purchase hardware and network infrastructure, provide travel grants to developer summits, and provide legal support to the FreeBSD project.[29]

License

FreeBSD is released under a variety of open source licenses. The kernel code and most newly created code is released under the two-clause BSD license which allows everyone to use and redistribute FreeBSD as they wish. There are parts released under three- and four-clause BSD licenses, as well as Beerware license. Some device drivers include a binary blob, such as the Atheros HAL of FreeBSD versions before 7.2.[30] Some of the code contributed by other projects is licensed under GPL, LGPL, ISC or CDDL. All the code licensed under GPL and CDDL is clearly separated from the code under liberal licenses, to make it easy for users such as embedded device manufacturers to use only permissive free software licenses. ClangBSD aims to replace some GPL dependencies in the FreeBSD base system by replacing the GNU compiler collection with the BSD-licenced LLVM/Clang compiler. ClangBSD became self-hosting on April 16, 2010,[31] an important landmark for further independent development.

Logo

For many years FreeBSD's logo was the generic BSD daemon, also called
Beastie, a slurred phonetic pronunciation of *BSD*. First appearing in 1976
on UNIX T-shirts purchased by Bell Labs, the more popular versions of the
BSD daemon were drawn by animation director John Lasseter beginning in
1984.[32] [33] [34] Several FreeBSD-specific versions were later drawn by
Tatsumi Hosokawa.[35] Through the years Beastie became both beloved
and criticized as perhaps inappropriate for corporate and mass market
exposure. Moreover it was not unique to FreeBSD. In lithographic terms,
the Lasseter graphic is not line art and often requires a screened, four
colour photo offset printing process for faithful reproduction on physical
surfaces such as paper. Moreover, the BSD daemon was thought to be too
graphically detailed for smooth size scaling and aesthetically over
dependent upon multiple colour gradations, making it hard to reliably

FreeBSD's mascot is the generic BSD
daemon, also known as *Beastie*.

reproduce as a simple, standardized logo in only two or three colours, much less in monochrome. Because of these
worries, a competition was held and a new logo designed by Anton K. Gural, still echoing the BSD daemon, was
released on October 8, 2005.[36] Meanwhile Lasseter's much known take on the BSD daemon carries forth as the
official mascot of the FreeBSD Project.

Derivatives

There are a number of software distributions based on FreeBSD
including:

- PC-BSD (aimed at home users and workstations)
- DesktopBSD (aimed at home users and workstations)
- FreeSBIE (live CD)
- Frenzy (live CD)
- GhostBSD (Gnome-based live CD)
- m0n0wall (firewall)
- pfSense (firewall)
- FreeNAS (for network attached storage)
- AuthServ (for network servers & storage)

PC-BSD

All these distributions have no or only minor changes when compared with the original FreeBSD base system. The
main difference to the original FreeBSD is that they come with pre-installed and pre-configured software for specific
use cases. This can be compared with Linux distributions, which are all binary compatible because they use the same
kernel and also use the same basic tools, compilers and libraries, while coming with different applications,
configurations and branding.

Besides these distributions there is DragonFly BSD, a fork from FreeBSD 4.8 aiming for a different multiprocessor
synchronization strategy than the one chosen for FreeBSD 5 and development of some microkernel features. It does
not aim to stay compatible with FreeBSD and has huge differences in the kernel and basic userland.

A wide variety of products are directly or indirectly based on FreeBSD. Examples of embedded devices based on
FreeBSD include:

- Citrix Netscalers
- F5 Networks's 3DNS version 3 global traffic manager and EDGE-FX version 1 web cache (NB These are now
  end of life with 3DNS functionality being moved to the Linux based BIGIP Platform)

- Ironport network security appliances
- Junos network operating system by Juniper Networks used in their routers, switches and security devices
- KACE Networks's KBOX 1000 & 2000 Series Appliances and the Virtual KBOX Appliance
- nCircle's IP360
- NetApp's Data ONTAP 8.x and the now superseded ONTAP GX (only as a loader for proprietary kernel-space module)
- Netasq security appliances
- Nokia's firewall operating system
- Panasas's and Isilon Systems's cluster storage operating systems
- The PlayStation 3 video game console.[37]
- Sandvine's network policy control products[38]
- Sophos's Email Appliance[39]
- St. Bernard Software iPrism web filtering appliances[40]
- Panasonic's 2010 TV models (PDP and LCD)
- Blue Coat's ProxySG WAN acceleration appliance is partially derived from FreeBSD[41]

Other operating systems such as Linux and the RTOS VxWorks contain code that originated in FreeBSD. Debian, known primarily for using the Linux kernel, also maintains GNU/kFreeBSD, combining the GNU userspace and C library with the FreeBSD kernel.[42] Darwin, the core of Apple OS X, borrows FreeBSD's virtual file system, network stack, and components of its userspace. The OpenDarwin project (now defunct), a spin-off of Apple's Darwin operating system, also included substantial FreeBSD code. Thanks to the permissive FreeBSD License [3], much of FreeBSD now also forms the basis of Apple OS X and OS X Server.

> Mac OS X Server includes the latest technological advances from the open source BSD community. Originally developed at the University of California, Berkeley, the BSD distribution is the foundation of most UNIX implementations today. Mac OS X Server is based largely on the FreeBSD distribution and includes the latest advances from this development community.
>
> —"Apple Mac OS X Server Snow Leopard — UNIX: Open source foundation", [43]

Installers

sysinstall

The sysinstall utility is the installation application provided by the FreeBSD Project. It uses a text user interface, and is divided into a number of menus and screens that can be used to configure and control the installation process. It can also be used to install Ports and Packages as an alternative to the command-line interface.[44] As of FreeBSD 9, sysinstall has been replaced by bsdinstall.

bsdinstall

The bsdinstall utility is a "a lightweight replacement for sysinstall",[45] and is intended to replace the sysinstall utility in FreeBSD 9.0.[46] bsdinstall is intended to be scriptable and extendable, with no dependencies outside the base system.

finstall

The finstall utility aims to create a user-friendly graphical installer for FreeBSD & FreeBSD-derived systems,[47] however development of finstall has stalled.[48]

Version history

FreeBSD 1

Released in November 1993. 1.1.5.1 was released in July, 1994.

FreeBSD 2

2.0-RELEASE was announced on November 22, 1994. The final release of FreeBSD 2, 2.2.8-RELEASE, was announced on November 29, 1998. FreeBSD 2.0 was the first FreeBSD to be claimed legally free of AT&T UNIX code with approval of Novell. It was the first version to be widely used at the beginnings of the spread of Internet servers.

FreeBSD 3

FreeBSD 3.0-RELEASE was announced on October 16, 1998. The final release, 3.5-RELEASE, was announced on June 24, 2000. FreeBSD 3.0 was the first branch able to support symmetric multiprocessing (SMP) systems, using a Giant lock. USB support was first introduced with FreeBSD 3.1, and the first Gigabit network cards were supported in 3.2-RELEASE.

FreeBSD 4

4.0-RELEASE appeared in March 2000 and the last 4-STABLE branch release was 4.11 in January 2005 supported until January 31, 2007.[49] FreeBSD 4 was lauded for its stability and was a favorite operating system for ISPs and web hosting providers during the first dot-com bubble, and is widely regarded as one of the most stable and high performance operating systems of the whole Unix lineage. Among the new features of FreeBSD 4, kqueue(2) was introduced (which is now part of other major BSD systems).

FreeBSD 5

After almost three years of development, the first 5.0-RELEASE in January 2003 was widely anticipated, featuring support for advanced multiprocessor and application threading, and for the UltraSPARC and IA-64 platforms. The first 5-STABLE release was 5.3 (5.0 through 5.2.1 were cut from *-CURRENT*). The last release from the 5-STABLE branch was 5.5 in May 2006.

The largest architectural development in FreeBSD 5 was a major change in the low-level kernel locking mechanisms to enable better symmetric multi-processor (SMP) support. This released much of the kernel from the MP lock, which is sometimes called the *Giant lock*. More than one process could now execute in kernel mode at the same time. Other major changes included an *M:N* native threading implementation called Kernel Scheduled Entities. In principle this is similar to Scheduler Activations. Starting with FreeBSD 5.3, KSE was the default threading implementation until it was replaced with a 1:1 implementation in FreeBSD 7.0.

FreeBSD 5 also significantly changed the block I/O layer by implementing the GEOM modular disk I/O request transformation framework contributed by Poul-Henning Kamp. GEOM enables the simple creation of many kinds of functionality, such as mirroring (gmirror) and encryption (GBDE and GELI). This work was supported through sponsorship by DARPA.

While the early versions from the 5.x were not much more than developer previews, with pronounced instability, the 5.4 and 5.5 releases of FreeBSD confirmed the technologies introduced in the FreeBSD 5.x branch had a future in highly stable and high-performing releases.

FreeBSD 6

FreeBSD 6.0 was released on November 4, 2005. The final FreeBSD 6 release was 6.4, on November 11, 2008. These versions continue work on SMP and threading optimization along with more work on advanced 802.11 functionality, TrustedBSD security event auditing, significant network stack performance enhancements, a fully preemptive kernel and support for hardware performance counters (HWPMC). The main accomplishments of these releases include removal of the Giant lock from VFS, implementation of a better-performing optional libthr library with 1:1 threading and the addition of a Basic Security Module (BSM) audit implementation called OpenBSM, which was created by the TrustedBSD Project (based on the BSM implementation found in Apple's open source Darwin) and released under a BSD-style license.

FreeBSD 7

FreeBSD 7.0 was released on 27 February 2008. The most recent and final FreeBSD 7 release was 7.4, on February 24, 2011. New features include SCTP, UFS journaling, an experimental port of Sun's ZFS file system, GCC4, improved support for the ARM architecture, jemalloc (a memory allocator optimized for parallel computation,[50] which was ported to Firefox 3),[51] and major updates and optimizations relating to network, audio, and SMP performance.[52] Benchmarks have shown significant speed improvements over previous FreeBSD releases as well as Linux.[53] The new ULE scheduler has seen much improvement but a decision was made to ship the 7.0 release with the older 4BSD scheduler, leaving ULE as a kernel compile-time tunable. In FreeBSD 7.1 ULE was the default for the i386 and AMD64 architectures.

Starting from version 7.1, DTrace was also integrated, and FreeBSD 7.2 brought support for multi-IPv4/IPv6 jails.[54]

Code supporting the DEC Alpha architecture (supported since FreeBSD 4.0) was removed in FreeBSD 7.0.[55]

FreeBSD 8

FreeBSD 8.0 was formally released on November 25, 2009.[56] FreeBSD 8.2 is the latest stable release of FreeBSD, having been branched from the trunk in December 2010. It features superpages, Xen DomU support, network stack virtualization, stack-smashing protection, TTY layer rewrite, much improved ZFS support, a new USB stack with USB 3.0 and xHCI support added in FreeBSD 8.2, multicast updates including IGMPv3, and rewritten NFS client/server introducing NFSv4, and AES acceleration on supported Intel CPUs (added in FreeBSD 8.2). Inclusion of improved device mmap() extensions enables implementation of a 64-bit Nvidia display driver for the x86-64 platform. FreeBSD 8.2 was formally released on February 24, 2011.[57]

FreeBSD 9

FreeBSD 9.0 was released on 12 January 2012. Key features of the release include a new installer (bsdinstall), UFS journaling, ZFS version 28, userland DTrace, NFSv4-compatible NFS server and client, USB 3.0 support, support for running on the PlayStation 3, Capsicum sandboxing, and LLVM 3.0 in the base system.[58] The kernel and base system can be built with Clang, but FreeBSD 9.0 still uses GCC4.2 by default.

Timeline

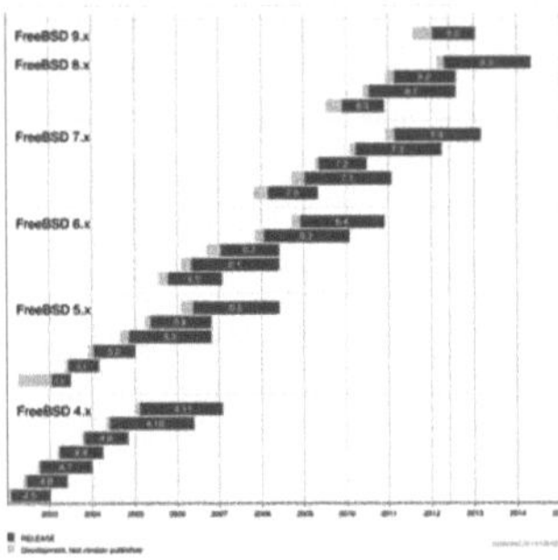

The timeline shows that the span of a single release generation of FreeBSD lasts around 5 years. Since the FreeBSD project makes effort for binary backward (and limited forward) compatibility within the same release generation,[59] this allows users 5+ years of support, with trivial-to-easy upgrading within the release generation.

See also

- BAPP - BSD + Apache + PostgreSQL + Perl/PHP/Python
- BSD descendants
- Commercial products based on FreeBSD
- Comparison of BSD operating systems
- Comparison of operating systems
- Comparison of operating system kernels
- Darwin (operating system) - a UNIX-like computer operating system released by Apple Inc and based largely on BSD.
- DragonFly BSD, a fork of FreeBSD.
- FreeBSD Documentation License
- FreeBSD Jail
- FreeBSD Ports
- GEOM
- Jordan Hubbard
- Linux
- Marshall Kirk McKusick
- NetBSD, another major freely licensed, open-source BSD derivative.
- OpenBSD, another major freely licensed, open-source BSD derivative (forked from NetBSD).
- Poul-Henning Kamp
- Robert Watson
- Security-focused operating system
- ULE scheduler

References

[1] http://en.wikipedia.org/wiki/Template%3Alatest_stable_software_release%2Ffreebsd

[2] http://en.wikipedia.org/wiki/Template%3Alatest_preview_software_release%2Ffreebsd

[3] http://www.freebsd.org/copyright/freebsd-license.html

[4] http://www.freebsd.org/copyright/freebsd-doc-license.html

[5] http://www.freebsd.org

[6] *USL v. BSDi et al.*

[7] Pohlmann, Frank. "Why FreeBSD" (http://www-128.ibm.com/developerworks/opensource/library/os-freebsd/). ibm.com. . Retrieved 2007-12-16.

[8] [IBSD Certification Group (http://www.bsdcertification.org/)] (31 October 2005) (PDF). *BSD Usage Survey* (http://www. bsdcertification.org/downloads/pr_20051031_usage_survey_en_en.pdf). The BSD Certification Group. . Retrieved 5 December 2010.

[9] "FreeBSD" (http://www.spreadbsd.org/?q=freebsd). spreadbsd.org. . Retrieved 2009-01-31.

[10] "Why FreeBSD" (http://www.ibm.com/developerworks/opensource/library/os-freebsd/). ibm.org. . Retrieved 2008-01-28.

[11] Lavigne, Dru (2004). *BSD Hacks.* O'Reilly Media. pp. 309. ISBN 978-0-596-00679-2.

[12] "A Brief History of FreeBSD" (http://www.freebsd.org/doc/en/books/handbook/history.html). freebsd.org. . Retrieved 2009-01-31.

[13] Hubbard, Jordan. "A Brief History of FreeBSD" (http://www.freebsd.org/doc/en_US.ISO8859-1/books/handbook/history.html). freebsd.org. . Retrieved 2007-12-16.

[14] McKusick, Marshall (2005). "Section 2.13". *The Design and Implementation of the FreeBSD Operating System.* ISBN 0-201-70245-2.

[15] "FreeBSD/Supported Platforms" (http://www.freebsd.org/platforms). freebsd.org. . Retrieved 2009-09-06.

[16] "Chapter 4 Installing Applications: Packages and Ports" (http://www.freebsd.org/doc/en_US.ISO8859-1/books/handbook/ports.html). freebsd.org. . Retrieved 2009-01-30.

[17] "4.5 Using the Ports Collection" (http://www.freebsd.org/doc/en_US.ISO8859-1/books/handbook/ports-using.html). freebsd.org. . Retrieved 2009-01-30.

[18] "4.4 Using the Packages System" (http://www.freebsd.org/doc/en_US.ISO8859-1/books/handbook/packages-using.html). freebsd.org. . Retrieved 2009-01-30.

[19] "FreeBSD Ports: Ports-mgmt" (http://www.freebsd.org/ports/ports-mgmt.html). freebsd.org. . Retrieved 2009-09-08.

[20] "Portmaster Home Page" (http://dougbarton.us/portmaster.html). Doug Barton. . Retrieved 2011-07-06.

[21] "portupgrade on the freebsd wiki" (http://wiki.freebsd.org/portupgrade). .

[22] "Chapter 10 Linux Binary Compatibility" (http://www.freebsd.org/doc/en_US.ISO8859-1/books/handbook/linuxemu.html). freebsd.org. . Retrieved 2007-03-29.

[23] Tiemann, Brian (2006). "How FreeBSD Compares to Other Operating Systems". *FreeBSD 6 Unleashed.* ISBN 0-672-32875-5.

[24] "Support for 64 Bit Linux binaries on FreeBSD (Mailing List)" (http://markmail.org/message/gsd3is7yz7w7sent). . Retrieved 2009-05-05.

[25] "List of FreeBSD developers" (http://www.freebsd.org/doc/en/articles/contributors/staff-committers.html). *Contributors to FreeBSD.* freebsd.org. . Retrieved 2010-03-13.

[26] "FreeBSD Project Administration and Management" (http://www.freebsd.org/administration.html). freebsd.org. . Retrieved 2009-01-30.

[27] "FAQ Chapter 1 Introduction" (http://www.freebsd.org/doc/en_US.ISO8859-1/books/faq/introduction.html). freebsd.org. . Retrieved 2009-01-30.

[28] Saers, Niklas (2002). "A project model for the FreeBSD Project" (http://www.freebsd.org/doc/en_US.ISO8859-1/books/dev-model/). freebsd.org. . Retrieved 2007-03-03.

[29] "About the FreeBSD Foundation" (http://www.freebsdfoundation.org/about.shtml). The FreeBSD Foundation. . Retrieved 2009-09-06.

[30] "FreeBSD Copyright and Legal Information" (http://www.freebsd.org/copyright/copyright.html). freebsd.org. . Retrieved 2009-01-30.

[31] "ClangBSD Is Selfhosting, We Need Testers Now" (http://www.osnews.com/story/23166/ClangBSD_Is_Selfhosting_We_Need_Testers_Now). osnews.com. 2010-04-17. . Retrieved 2010-05-13.

[32] "Usenix" (http://www.mckusick.com/beastie/shirts/usenix.html). mckusick.com. . Retrieved 2007-12-15.

[33] "Saving UNIX from /dev/null" (http://minnie.tuhs.org/Seminars/Saving_Unix/). minnie.tuhs.org. . Retrieved 2007-12-15.

[34] "Chuck's Corner" (http://www.frbsd.org/fr/chuck.html). frbsd.org. . Retrieved 2007-12-19.

[35] "The BSD Daemon" (http://www.freebsd.org/copyright/daemon.html). freebsd.org. . Retrieved 2007-12-15.

[36] "Final result for the FreeBSD logo design competition" (http://logo-contest.freebsd.org/result/). freebsd.org. 2005. . Retrieved 2007-03-01.

[37] "Licenses of software used on PlayStation®3 console" (http://www.scei.co.jp/ps3-license/index.html). . Retrieved 11 August 2010.

[38] Maste, Ed. "FreeBSD at Sandvine" (http://www.bsdcan.org/2011/schedule/events/232.en.html). *BSDCan 2011.* .

[39] "Sophos Email Appliance: overview" (http://www.sophos.com/support/knowledgebase/article/14384.html). .

[40] "iPrism v6.2xx" (http://www.stbernard.com/docs/releasenotes/iPrism_6-2xx.pdf). .

[41] Sean Michael Kerner (21 August 2009). "FreeBSD 8 Getting New Routing Architecture" (http://www.internetnews.com/dev-news/article.php/3835746). internetnews.com. . Retrieved 19 December 2010.

[42] "Debian GNU/kFreeBSD" (http://www.debian.org/ports/kfreebsd-gnu/). . Retrieved 11 August 2010.

[43] http://www.apple.com/server/macosx/technology/unix.html

[44] "2.5 Introducing Sysinstall" (http://www.freebsd.org/doc/en/books/handbook/using-sysinstall.html). freebsd.org. . Retrieved
     2009-01-30.
[45] "BSDInstall: The Stopgap Installer" (http://wiki.freebsd.org/BSDInstall). .
[46] "bsdinstall - testers wanted" (http://forums.freebsd.org/showthread.php?t=20857). Joel Dahl. .
[47] "The finstall project" (http://wiki.freebsd.org/finstall). freebsd.org. . Retrieved 2009-01-30.
[48] "What happened to finstall?" (http://ivoras.sharanet.org/blog/tree/2009-02-19.what-happened-to-finstall.html). Ivan Voras. . Retrieved
     2009-03-17.
[49] "FreeBSD 4.x EoL announcement" (http://lists.freebsd.org/pipermail/freebsd-security/2006-October/004111.html). .
[50] Evans, Jason (2006-04-16). "A Scalable Concurrent malloc(3) Implementation for FreeBSD" (http://people.freebsd.org/~jasone/
     jemalloc/bsdcan2006/jemalloc.pdf) (PDF). . Retrieved 2008-02-13.
[51] "FreeBSD 7.0-RELEASE Announcement" (http://www.freebsd.org/releases/7.0R/announce.html). freebsd.org. . Retrieved
     2009-01-31.
[52] Biancuzzi, Federico (2008-02-26). "What's New in FreeBSD 7.0" (http://www.onlamp.com/pub/a/bsd/2008/02/26/
     whats-new-in-freebsd-70.html?page=1). onlamp.com. . Retrieved 2008-02-26.
[53] "Introducing FreeBSD 7.0" (http://people.freebsd.org/~kris/scaling/7.0 Preview.pdf). freebsd.org. . Retrieved 2009-01-31.
[54] "FreeBSD 7.2-RELEASE Announcement" (http://www.freebsd.org/releases/7.2R/announce.html). freebsd.org. . Retrieved
     2009-05-04.
[55] "FreeBSD 7.0-RELEASE Release Notes" (http://www.freebsd.org/releases/7.0R/relnotes.html). freebsd.org. . Retrieved 2009-05-03.
[56] "FreeBSD Project Announces Release of FreeBSD Version 8.0" (http://www.freebsd.org/releases/8.0R/pressrelease.html). The
     FreeBSD Project. 2009-11-25. . Retrieved 2009-11-27.
[57] "FreeBSD 8.2-RELEASE Announcement" (http://www.freebsd.org/releases/8.2R/announce.html). The FreeBSD Project. 24 February
     2011. . Retrieved 2011-02-24.
[58] "FreeBSD Project Announces Release of FreeBSD Version 9.0" (http://www.freebsd.org/releases/9.0R/announce.html). The FreeBSD
     Project. 2012-01-12. . Retrieved 2012-01-12.
[59] FreeBSD Handbook information on upgrading (http://www.freebsd.org/doc/en_US.ISO8859-1/books/handbook/current-stable.html)

Notes

- Negus, Christopher; Caen, Francois (May 5, 2008). *BSD UNIX Toolbox: 1000+ Commands for FreeBSD,
  OpenBSD and NetBSD* (http://eu.wiley.com/WileyCDA/WileyTitle/productCd-0470376031.html) (First ed.).
  Wiley. pp. 309. ISBN 0-470-37603-1
- Lavigne, Dru (May 24, 2004). *BSD Hacks* (http://oreilly.com/catalog/9780596006792/) (First ed.). O'Reilly
  Media. pp. 448. ISBN 0-596-00679-9
- Lucas, Michael W. (November 14, 2007). *Absolute FreeBSD* (http://nostarch.com/abs_bsd2.htm) (Second ed.).
  No Starch Press. pp. 744. ISBN 1-59327-151-4
- Lavigne, Dru; Lehey, Greg; Reed, Jeremy C. (December 20, 2007). *The Best of FreeBSD Basics* (http://www.
  reedmedia.net/books/freebsd-basics/) (First ed.). Reed Media Services. pp. 596. ISBN 0-9790342-2-1
- Hong, Bryan J. (April 1, 2008). *Building a Server with FreeBSD 7* (http://nostarch.com/freebsdserver.htm)
  (First ed.). No Starch Press. pp. 288. ISBN 978-1-59327-145-9
- Tiemann, Brian; Urban, Michael (June 15, 2006). *FreeBSD 6 Unleashed* (http://www.informit.com/store/
  product.aspx?isbn=0-672-32875-5) (First ed.). Sams. pp. 912. ISBN 0-672-32875-5
- Korff, Yanek; Hope, Paco; Potter, Bruce (March 2005). *Mastering FreeBSD and OpenBSD Security* (http://
  oreilly.com/catalog/9780596006266) (First ed.). O'Reilly Media. pp. 464. ISBN 0-596-00626-8
- Lehey, Greg (April 2003). *The Complete FreeBSD* (http://oreilly.com/catalog/9780596005160) (Fourth ed.).
  O'Reilly Media. pp. 720. ISBN 0-596-00516-4
- McKusick, Marshall K.; Neville-Neil, George V. (August 2, 2004). *The Design and Implementation of the
  FreeBSD Operating System* (http://www.informit.com/store/product.aspx?isbn=0201702452) (First ed.).
  Addison−Wesley. pp. 720. ISBN 0-201-70245-2
- Mittelstaedt, Ted (December 15, 2000). *The FreeBSD Corporate Networker's Guide* (http://www.freebsd.org/
  doc/en/books/corp-net-guide/index.html) (First ed.). Addison−Wesley. pp. 432. ISBN 0-201-70481-1
- Stokely, Murray; Lee, Chern (March 1, 2004). *The FreeBSD Handbook, Volume 1: User Guide* (http://www.
  freebsdmall.com/cgi-bin/fm/bsdhandbk3.1) (Third ed.). FreeBSD Mall. pp. 408. ISBN 1-57176-327-9

- Stokely, Murray (September 1, 2004). *The FreeBSD Handbook, Volume 2: Admin Guide* (http://www.freebsdmall.com/cgi-bin/fm/bsdhandbk3.2) (Third ed.). FreeBSD Mall. pp. 537. ISBN 1-57176-328-7

External links

- Official website (http://http://www.freebsd.org/)
- Official Forums (http://forums.freebsd.org/)
- Official Wiki (http://wiki.freebsd.org)
- Official FreeBSD Handbook (http://www.freebsd.org/doc/en_US.ISO8859-1/books/handbook/)
- *FreeBSD* (http://distrowatch.com/table.php?distribution=freebsd) at DistroWatch

PC-BSD

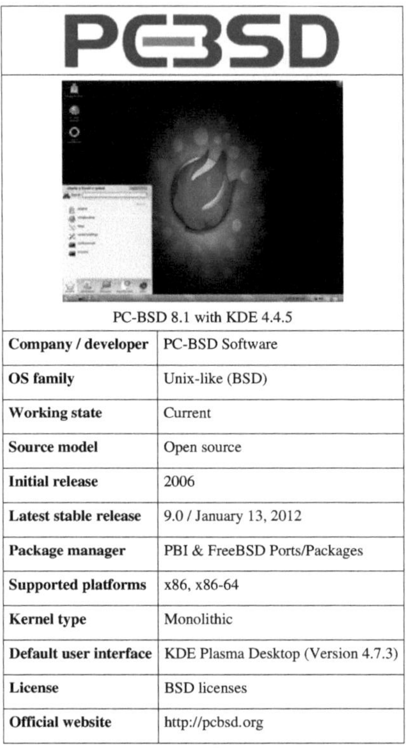

PC-BSD 8.1 with KDE 4.4.5

Company / developer	PC-BSD Software
OS family	Unix-like (BSD)
Working state	Current
Source model	Open source
Initial release	2006
Latest stable release	9.0 / January 13, 2012
Package manager	PBI & FreeBSD Ports/Packages
Supported platforms	x86, x86-64
Kernel type	Monolithic
Default user interface	KDE Plasma Desktop (Version 4.7.3)
License	BSD licenses
Official website	http://pcbsd.org

PC-BSD, or **PCBSD**, is a Unix-like, desktop-oriented operating system built upon the most recent releases of FreeBSD. It aims to be easy to install by using a graphical installation program, and easy and ready-to-use immediately by providing KDE SC as the pre-installed graphical user interface. It provides official binary nVidia and Intel drivers for hardware acceleration and an optional 3D desktop interface through Kwin, and Wine is ready-to-use in running Microsoft Windows software. PC-BSD is able to run Linux software, in addition to FreeBSD ports, and it has its own PBI package management system that allows users to graphically install pre-built software packages from a single downloaded executable file, which is unique for BSD operating systems.

PC-BSD supports ZFS, and the installer offers disk encryption with geli so the system will require a passphrase before booting.

History

PC-BSD was originally founded by FreeBSD professional Kris Moore in early 2005. In August 2006 it was voted the most beginner friendly operating system by OSWeekly.com.[1]

The first Beta consisted of only a GUI installer to get the user up and running with a FreeBSD 6 system with KDE3 pre-configured. This was a major innovation for the time as anyone wishing to install FreeBSD would have to manually tweak and run through a text installer. Kris Moore's goal was to make FreeBSD easy for everyone to use on the desktop and has since diverged even more in the direction of usability by including additional GUI administration tools and PBI packages (see Package management).

Since October 10, 2006 PC-BSD has been supported by the enterprise-class hardware solution provider iXsystems.[2] [3] iXsystems now employs Mr. Moore as a full time developer and leader of the project. In November 2007, iXsystems entered into a distribution agreement with Fry's Electronics whereby Fry's Electronics stores nationwide carry boxed copies of PC-BSD version 1.4 (Da Vinci Edition).[4] In January 2008, iXsystems entered into a similar agreement with Micro Center.[5]

Release history

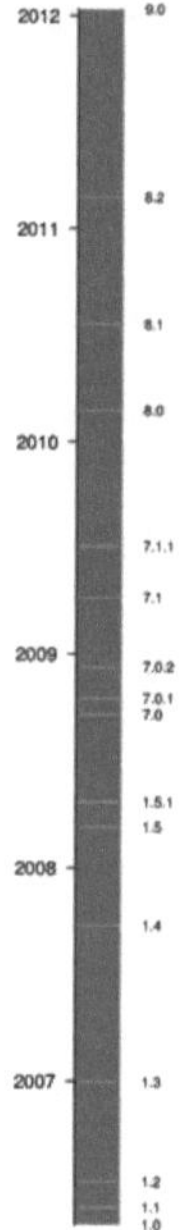

Version	Release date	FreeBSD codebase
1.0	April 29, 2006	6.0
1.1	May 29, 2006	6.1
1.2	July 12, 2006	6.1
1.3	December 31, 2006	6.1
1.4	September 24, 2007	6.2-STABLE
1.4.1.x	Various	6.3-PRERELEASE
1.5	March 12, 2008	6.3-STABLE
1.5.1	April 23, 2008	6.3-STABLE
7.0	September 16, 2008	7.0-STABLE
7.0.1	October 17, 2008	7.0-STABLE
7.0.2	December 10, 2008	7.1-PRERELEASE
7.1-BETA1	March 6, 2009	7.1-RELEASE
7.1-RC1	March 27, 2009	7.2-PRERELEASE
7.1	April 10, 2009	7.2-PRERELEASE
7.1.1	July 6, 2009	7.2-STABLE
8.0-BETA	January 1, 2010	8.0-RELEASE
8.0-RC1	January 27, 2010	8.0-RELEASE-P2
8.0-RC2	February 11, 2010	8.0-RELEASE-P2
8.0	February 23, 2010	8.0-RELEASE-P2
8.1-BETA1	June 6, 2010	8.1-PRERELEASE
8.1-RC1	June 21, 2010	8.1-RC1
8.1	July 21, 2010	8.1-RELEASE
9.0-ALPHA1	November 4, 2010	9.0-CURRENT [6]
9.0-ALPHA2	December 6, 2010	9.0-CURRENT [7]
8.2-BETA1	December 6, 2010	8.2-PRERELEASE [8]
8.2-RC1	January 10, 2011	8.2-RC1 [9]
9.0-ALPHA3	January 17, 2011	9.0-CURRENT [10]
8.2-RC2	January 20, 2011	8.2-RC2 [11]
8.2-RC3	February 3, 2011	8.2-RC3 [12]
8.2	February 24, 2011	8.2 [13]
9.0-BETA1	August 1, 2011	9.0-BETA1 [14]
9.0-BETA1.5	August 19, 2011	9.0-BETA1.5 [15]
9.0-BETA2	September 13, 2011	9.0-BETA2 [16]
9.0-BETA3	October 2, 2011	9.0-BETA3 [17]
9.0-RC1	October 24, 2011	9.0-RC1 [18]

9.0-RC2	November 23, 2011	9.0-RC2 [19]
9.0-RC3	December 13, 2011	9.0-RC3 [20]
9.0	January 13, 2012	9.0 [21]

Since version 7, PC-BSD began following the same numbering system as FreeBSD. PC-BSD exclusively used KDE SC, until version 9.0, which has been customized to support tighter application integration and the PBI package management system. While manual installation of other desktops such as Xfce and GNOME was technically possible, none of these were supported and major functionality was lost when not using PC-BSD's special build of KDE SC.[22] GNOME is offered, including Xfce, LXDE and other DEs, starting with PC-BSD 9.0.

PC-BSD supports x86 and x86-64 architectures.

Package management

PC-BSD's package management system takes a different approach to installing software than many other Unix-like operating systems. Instead of using the FreeBSD ports tree directly (although it remains available), PC-BSD uses files with the *.pbi* filename extension which, when double-clicked, bring up an installation wizard program. An autobuild system tracks the FreeBSD ports collection and generates new PBIs daily. The generated PBIs are maintained at the PC-BSD software repository [23].

All software packages and dependencies are installed in their own self-contained directories in */Programs*. This convention is aimed to decrease confusion about where binary programs reside, remove the possibility of a package breaking if system libraries are upgraded or changed, and prevent dependency hell. The PC-BSD package manager also takes care of creating categorized links in the KDE menu and on the KDE SC desktop.

The PC-BSD package management system aims to be similar to that of major operating systems such as Microsoft Windows and Apple Mac OS X, where applications are installed from a single downloaded file with graphical prompts, rather than the traditional package management systems that many Unix-like systems use.

License

PC-BSD was originally licensed under the GNU General Public License (GPL) because the developers were under the impression that applications using the Qt, which PC-BSD uses for its interface development, must be licensed under the GPL or the QPL. Upon discovering that there was no such restriction in fact, the PC-BSD developers later relicensed the code under a BSD-like license. In March 2009 Qt added an LGPL License.

PC-BSD 8.x Requirements

Minimum system requirements[24] :

- Intel Pentium II or higher
- 512 MB RAM
- 12 GB of free Hard Drive space (Primary partition or entire disk)
- Network card
- Sound card

Recommended system requirements:

- Intel Pentium 4 or higher
- 1 GB of RAM
- 20 GB of free Hard Drive space (Primary partition or entire disk)
- Network card

- Sound card
- 3D accelerated video card (NVIDIA, ATI)

Though 512 MB RAM is the absolute minimum, one should use at least 1 GB of RAM if possible. To play modern video games, a fast CPU is recommended, and to create a collection of music and videos, a larger hard disk drive is recommended. To use ZFS, 1 GB of RAM is required. 4 GB RAM is recommended for advanced features such as ZFS deduplication, but ZFS will use as much additional RAM as can be provided.

See also

- Comparison of BSD operating systems

References

- Kerner, Sean Michael (October 12, 2006). "FreeBSD based PC-BSD Gets 'Acquired'" [25]. internetnews.com.
- Kerner, Sean Michael (January 2, 2007). "New Year, New Look For PC-BSD" [26]. internetnews.com.

[1] "The Most Beginner Friendly OS" (http://www.osweekly.com/index.php?option=com_content&task=view&id=2287&Itemid=449). . Retrieved 2006-08-10.

[2] "iXsystems Announces Acquisition of PC-BSD Operating System" (http://www.ixsystems.com/ix/media/ ixsystems-announces-acquisition-of-pc-bsd-operating-system). *iXsystems.com*. . Retrieved 2011-06-29.

[3] Mayank Sharma (2006-10-13). "Why iXsystems bought PC-BSD" (http://www.linux.com/archive/feature/57794?theme=print). *linux.com*. . Retrieved 2010-04-01.

[4] "iXsystems Announces Distribution Agreement with Fry's Electronics" (http://www.ixsystems.com/ix/media/ ixsystems-announces-distribution-agreement-with-frys-electronics-for-pc-bsd). . Retrieved 2011-06-29.

[5] "iXsystems Announces Distribution Agreement with Micro Center for PC-BSD" (http://www.ixsystems.com/ix/media/ ixsystems-announces-distribution-agreement-with-micro-center-for-pc-bsd). . Retrieved 2011-06-29.

[6] "First 9.0 Alpha Snapshot Available for Testing" (http://blog.pcbsd.org/2010/11/first-9-0-alpha-snapshot-available-for-testing/). . Retrieved 2010-11-04.

[7] "Latest 9.0 Snapshot is Available for Testing" (http://blog.pcbsd.org/2010/12/latest-9-0-snapshot-is-available-for-testing/). . Retrieved 2010-12-06.

[8] "First 8.2 Snapshot is Available for Testing" (http://blog.pcbsd.org/2010/12/first-8-2-snapshot-is-available-for-testing/). . Retrieved 2010-12-07.

[9] "PC-BSD 8.2-RC1 Available for Testing" (http://blog.pcbsd.org/2011/01/pc-bsd-8-2-rc1-available-for-testing/). . Retrieved 2011-01-10.

[10] "Next 9.0 Snapshot is Available for Testing" (http://blog.pcbsd.org/2011/01/next-9-0-snapshot-is-available-for-testing/). . Retrieved 2011-01-17.

[11] "PC-BSD 8.2-RC2 Available for Testing" (http://blog.pcbsd.org/2011/01/pc-bsd-8-2-rc2-available-for-testing/). . Retrieved 2011-01-20.

[12] "PC-BSD 8.2-RC3 Now Available!" (http://blog.pcbsd.org/2011/02/pc-bsd-8-2-rc3-now-available/). . Retrieved 2011-02-03.

[13] "PC-BSD 8.2 Released" (http://blog.pcbsd.org/2011/02/pc-bsd-8-2-released/). . Retrieved 2011-02-24.

[14] "Release Announcement: PC-BSD 9.0-BETA1" (http://blog.pcbsd.org/2011/08/release-announcement-pc-bsd-9-0-beta1/). . Retrieved 2011-08-01.

[15] "PC-BSD 9.0-BETA1.5 Available for Testing" (http://blog.pcbsd.org/2011/08/pc-bsd-9-0-beta1-5-available-for-testing/). . Retrieved 2011-08-19.

[16] "PC-BSD 9.0-BETA2 Available for Testing" (http://blog.pcbsd.org/2011/09/pc-bsd-9-0-beta2-available-for-testing/). . Retrieved 2011-09-13.

[17] "PC-BSD BETA3 Available" (http://blog.pcbsd.org/2011/10/pc-bsd-beta3-available/). . Retrieved 2011-10-02.

[18] "PC-BSD 9.0RC1 Available" (http://blog.pcbsd.org/2011/10/pc-bsd-9-0rc1-available/). . Retrieved 2011-10-24.

[19] "PC-BSD 9.0RC2 now Available" (http://blog.pcbsd.org/2011/11/pc-bsd-9-0-rc2-now-available/). . Retrieved 2011-11-23.

[20] "PC-BSD 9.0RC3 now Available" (http://blog.pcbsd.org/2011/12/pc-bsd-9-0-rc3-now-available/). . Retrieved 2011-12-13.

[21] "PC-BSD 9.0 Released!" (http://blog.pcbsd.org/2012/01/pc-bsd-9-0-released/). . Retrieved 2012-01-13.

[22] "Can I use Gnome with PC-BSD?" (http://faqs.pcbsd.org/index.php?action=artikel&cat=8&id=334&artlang=en). *PC-BSD knowledge base*. . Retrieved 2009-03-05.

[23] http://www.pbidir.com/

[24] "Minimum requirement from Users handbook." (http://wiki.pcbsd.org/index.php/Minimum_Hardware_Requirements). .

[25] http://www.internetnews.com/dev-news/article.php/3637341

[26] http://www.internetnews.com/dev-news/article.php/3651641

External links

- Official website (http://www.pcbsd.org/)
- PC-BSD software repository (http://pbidir.com)
- PC-BSD Forums (http://forums.pcbsd.org)
- Interview with Kris Moore on DistroWatch (http://distrowatch.com/weekly.php?issue=20080825#feature)
- Interview with Kris Moore on FLOSS Weekly (http://twit.tv/show/floss-weekly/182)

DesktopBSD

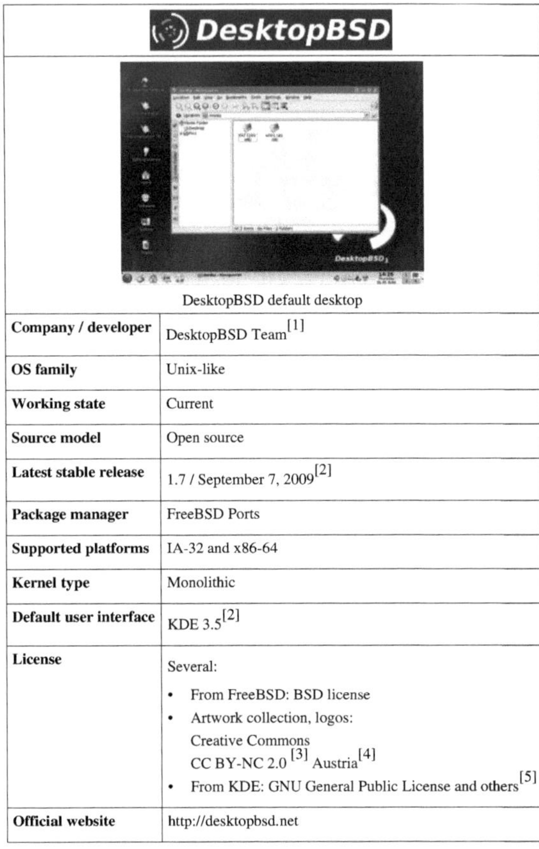

DesktopBSD default desktop

Company / developer	DesktopBSD Team[1]
OS family	Unix-like
Working state	Current
Source model	Open source
Latest stable release	1.7 / September 7, 2009[2]
Package manager	FreeBSD Ports
Supported platforms	IA-32 and x86-64
Kernel type	Monolithic
Default user interface	KDE 3.5[2]
License	Several: • From FreeBSD: BSD license • Artwork collection, logos: Creative Commons CC BY-NC 2.0 [3] Austria[4] • From KDE: GNU General Public License and others[5]
Official website	http://desktopbsd.net

DesktopBSD is a Unix-derivative, desktop-oriented operating system based on FreeBSD. Its goal is to combine the stability of FreeBSD with the ease-of-use of KDE, which is the default graphical user interface.

History and development

DesktopBSD is essentially a customized installation of FreeBSD and is not a fork of FreeBSD. DesktopBSD is always based on FreeBSD's latest stable branch but incorporates certain customized, pre-installed software such as KDE and DesktopBSD utilities and configuration files.

A common misconception about DesktopBSD is that it is intended as a rival to PC-BSD as a BSD-based desktop distribution, since they are similar in structure and goals. However, the DesktopBSD project was started approximately one year before the PC-BSD project, despite the fact that the first PC-BSD release came out before DesktopBSD's. Neither the DesktopBSD nor PC-BSD projects intend to rival each other and are completely independent projects with distinctive features and intended outcomes: e.g., DesktopBSD uses ports and packages for additional software installation, whereas PC-BSD introduced PBIs.

The current release is 1.7 which was made available on September 7, 2009. The release announcement stated "This is *the last and final release* of the DesktopBSD project" because the lead developer could no longer contribute the time required to maintain it.[6] As of May 2010 development of DesktopBSD has been restarted under new leadership.

However, development and announcements seem to have stopped and Desktop BSD appears to be a dead release.

Features

- Graphical installer allowing to partition disks and create users
- Graphical tool for managing, installing and updating software using FreeBSD ports system
- Graphical management of network interfaces and mounting/unmounting drives

1.7 Release

The 1.7 Release includes

- FreeBSD 7.2 as base system
- OpenOffice.org 3.1.1 as feature-rich office suite
- Pre-installed Java SE 6 environment
- X.Org release 7.4 with extensive graphics support
- Large number of enhancements, fixes and minor software updates
- Supports GRUB bootloader on i386 and includes a graphical configuration tool

On 7 September 2009 DesktopBSD 1.7 was made available on the project site.[7]

See also

- Comparison of BSD operating systems
- FreeBSD

References

[1] "DesktopBSD Team Members" (http://desktopbsd.net/wiki/doku.php?id=team:team). *desktopbsd.net.* . Retrieved 2010-04-01.

[2] "DistroWatch: DesktopBSD" (http://distrowatch.com/desktopbsd). *distrowatch.com.* . Retrieved 2011-10-18.

[3] http://creativecommons.org/licenses/by-nc/2.0/

[4] "DesktopBSD Artwork Collection" (http://desktopbsd.net/index.php?id=76). *desktopbsd.net.* . Retrieved 2008-03-20.

[5] "KDE Licensing Policy" (http://techbase.kde.org/index.php?title=Policies/Licensing_Policy). *KDE TechBase.* . Retrieved 2010-04-01.

[6] "DesktopBSD 1.7 available" (http://desktopbsd.net/index.php?id=43&tx_ttnews[tt_news]=41&cHash=b6ad95fd57). *desktopbsd.net.* 2009-09-07. . Retrieved 2009-09-27.

[7] "DesktopBSD 1.7 release notes" (http://desktopbsd.net/index.php?id=94). *desktopbsd.net.* 2009-09-07. . Retrieved 2011-10-18.

External links

- DesktopBSD homepage (http://desktopbsd.net/), wiki (http://desktopbsd.net/wiki/doku.php) and developer blog (http://desktopbsd.net/blog)
- DesktopBSD 1.0 release notes (http://www.desktopbsd.net/index.php?id=71)
- BSDTalk (http://bsdtalk.blogspot.com/2006/04/bsdtalk031-interview-with-peter-hofer.html) Interview with Peter Hofer (DesktopBSD developer/mp3)
- DesktopBSD flyer (http://www.allbsd.de/src/Flyer/FreeBSD/PDF/flyer-en-fbsd-desktopbsd.pdf) Info from AllBSD.de (http://www.allbsd.de/) (pdf/English)
- Using DesktopBSD (http://www.onlamp.com/pub/a/bsd/2006/07/13/FreeBSDBasics.html?page=1) Dru Lavigne

GNUstep

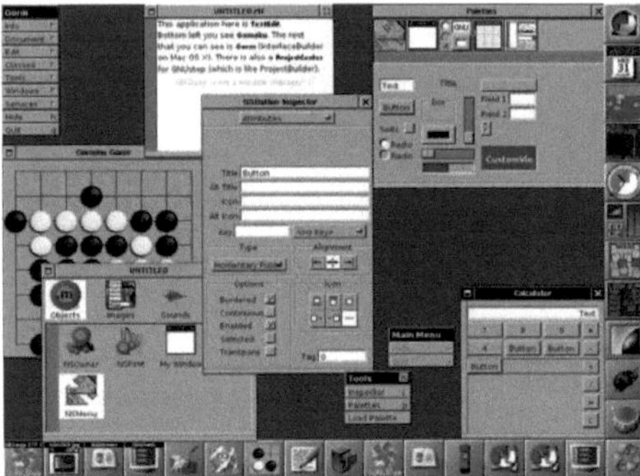

GNUstep screenshot, showing a variety of applications developed with the GNUstep libraries, including a gomoku game, calculator, and a text editor.

Developer(s)	GNUstep Developers
Stable release	make 2.6.0, base 1.22.0, gui & back 0.20.0 / April 15, 2011 (make April 15, 2011)
Preview release	make 2.6.0, base 1.21.0, gui & back 0.19.0 / May 10, 2010 (make May 8, 2010)
Written in	Objective-C
Operating system	Cross-platform
Type	Widget toolkit
License	GNU General Public License for the applications GNU Lesser General Public License for the libraries.
Website	www.gnustep.org [1]

GNUstep is a free software implementation of Cocoa (formerly NeXT's OpenStep) Objective-C libraries (called *frameworks*), widget toolkit, and application development tools not only for Unix-like operating systems, but also for Microsoft Windows. It is part of the GNU Project.

GNUstep features a cross-platform, object-oriented development environment. Like Apple Cocoa, GNUstep also has a Java interface, as well as Ruby,[2] Guile and Scheme[3] bindings. The GNUstep developers track some additions to Apple's Cocoa to remain compatible. The roots of the GNUstep application interface are the same as the roots of Cocoa: NeXT and OpenStep. GNUstep predates Cocoa.

History

GNUstep began when Paul Kunz and others at Stanford Linear Accelerator Center wanted to port HippoDraw from NEXTSTEP to another platform. Instead of rewriting HippoDraw from scratch and reusing only the application design, they decided to rewrite the NeXTSTEP object layer on which the application depended. This was the first version of *libobjcX*. It enabled them to port HippoDraw to Unix systems running the X Window System without changing a single line of their application source. After the OpenStep specification was released to the public in

1994, they decided to write a new *objcX* which would adhere to the new APIs. The software would become known as "GNUstep".[4]

Paradigms

GNUstep inherits some design principles proposed in Cocoa (formerly OPENSTEP) as well as the Objective-C language.

*   Model-view-controller paradigm
*   Target-Action
*   Drag-and-drop
*   Delegation
*   Message forwarding (through NSInvocation)

Applications

Here are some examples of applications written for or ported to GNUstep.

Written from scratch

*   Addresses
*   GNUMail, an e-mail client
*   GNUstep Database Library 2, an Enterprise Objects Framework clone
*   GNUstepWeb, an application server
*   Gorm, an interface builder
*   GWorkspace, a workspace and file manager
*   Grr, an RSS feed reader
*   Oolite, a clone of *Elite*, a space strategy game
*   PRICE, imaging application
*   ProjectCenter, the Project Builder or Xcode equivalent.
*   TalkSoup
*   Terminal
*   Zipper

Ported from NeXTSTEP, OPENSTEP, or Mac OS X

*   Adun
*   BioCocoa
*   Chess
*   Cenon
*   EdenMath
*   Eggplant
*   Emacs
*   Fortunate
*   Gomoku
*   NeXTGO
*   TextEdit
*   TimeMon

Class capabilities

Foundation Kit

* strings
* collections (arrays, sets, dictionaries) and enumerators
* file management
* object archiving
* advanced date manipulation
* distributed objects and inter-process communication
* URL handling
* notifications (and distributed notifications)
* easy multi-threading
* timers
* locks
* exception handling

Application Kit

* user interface elements (table views, browsers, matrices, scroll views)
* graphics (WYSIWYG, postscript-like graphics, bezier paths, image handling with multiple representations, graphical contexts)
* color management (calibrated vs. device colors; CMYK, RGB, HSB, gray and named color representations; alpha transparency)
* text system features: rich text format, text attachments, layout manager, typesetter, rules, paragraph styles, font management, spelling
* document management
* printing features: print operations, print panel and page layout
* help manager
* pasteboard (aka clip board) services
* spell checker
* workspace bindings for applications
* drag and drop operations
* services sharing among applications

See also

* Étoilé - GNUstep-based desktop environment
* GNUstep Renaissance - framework for XML description of portable GNUstep/Mac OS X user interfaces
* Miller Columns The method of file tree browsing the GWorkspace File Viewer uses
* Property list - often used file format to store user settings
* StepTalk - Scripting framework
* Window Maker - a window manager designed to emulate the NeXT GUI as part of the wider GNUstep project

References

[1] http://www.gnustep.org/

[2] GNUstep Developer Tools - RIGS (http://www.gnustep.org/experience/RIGS.html)

[3] GScheme (http://gnustep.it/marko/GScheme)

[4] GNUstep history (http://gnustep.made-it.com/Guides/History.html)

External links

- GNUstep.org (http://www.gnustep.org/) project homepage
- GNUstep Applications and Developer Tutorials (http://www.gnustep.it)
- The GNUstep Application Project (http://gap.nongnu.org/)
- A 2003 interview with GNUstep developer Nicola Pero (http://www.network-theory.co.uk/articles/pero. html)
- FLOSS Weekly Interview with Gregory Casamento and Riccardo Mottola from GNUstep (http://twit.tv/ floss44)

Release_engineering

Release engineering, frequently abbreviated as "ER", is a sub-discipline in software engineering concerned with the compilation, assembly, and delivery of source code into finished products or other software components. Associated with the software release life cycle, it is often said that release engineering is to software engineering as manufacturing is to an industrial process. While it is not the goal of release engineering to encumber software development with a process overlay, it is often seen as a sign of organizational and developmental maturity.

Modern release engineering is concerned with several aspects of software production:

Identifiability

> Being able to identify all of the source, tools, environment, and other components that make up a particular release

Reproducibility

> the ability to integrate source, third party components, data, and deployment externals of a software system in order to guarantee operational stability.

Consistency

> the mission to provide a stable framework for development, deployment, audit and accountability for software components.

Agility

> the ongoing research into what are the repercussions of modern software engineering practices on the productivity in the software cycle, i.e. continuous integration and push on green initiatives.

Release engineering is often the integration hub for more complex software development teams, sitting at the cross between development, product management, quality assurance and other engineering efforts, also known as DevOps. Release engineering teams are often cast in the role of gatekeepers (i.e. at Facebook, Google, Microsoft) for certain critical products where their judgement forms a parallel line of responsibility and authority in relation to production releases (pushes).

Frequently, tracking of changes in a configuration management system or revision control system is part of the domain of the release engineer. The responsibility for creating and applying a version numbering scheme into software—and tracking that number back to the specific source files to which it applies—often falls onto the release engineer. Producing or improving automation in software production is usually a goal of the release engineer.

Gathering, tracking, and supplying all the tools that are required to develop and build a particular piece of software may be a release engineering task, in order to reliably reproduce or maintain software years after its initial release to customers.

While most software engineers, or software developers, do many or all of the above as a course of their work, in larger organizations the specialty of the release engineer can be applied to coordinate disparate source trees, projects, teams, and components. This frees the developers to implement features in the software and also frees the quality assurance engineers to more broadly and deeply test the produced software.

The release engineer may provide software, services, or both to software engineering and software quality assurance teams. The software provided may be build tools, assembly, or other reorganization scripts which take compilation output and place them into a pre-defined tree structure, and even to the authoring and creation of installers for use by test teams or by the ultimate consumer of the software. The services provided may include software build (compilation) automation, automated test integration, results reporting, and production of or preparation for software delivery systems—e.g., in the form of electronic media (CDs, DVDs) or electronic software distribution mechanisms.

Related disciplines

- Build automation
- Porting - Product Line Engineering includes porting of a software product from one platform to other.
- Software configuration management - Although release engineering is sometimes considered part of Software Configuration Management, the latter, being a tool or a process used by the Release Engineer, is actually more of a subset of the roles and responsibilities of the typical Release Engineer.
- Continuous integration
- Change management
- Release management
- Packaging & Deployment

References

Further reading

- "Software Release Methodology" by Michael E. Bays; ISBN 0-13-636564-7.
- "Software Configuration Management" by H. Ronald Berlack; ISBN 0-471-53049-2.
- "Design of a Methodology to Support Software Release Decisions" by H. Sassenburg; ISBN 90-367-2424-4.
- "Continuous Delivery: Reliable Software Releases through Build, Test, and Deployment Automation" by Jez Humble, David Farley; ISBN 0-321-60191-2

Portable_C_Compiler

Stable release	1.0 / April 1, 2011
Written in	C
Operating system	Unix-like
Type	C Compiler
License	BSD License
Website	pcc.ludd.ltu.se [1]

The **Portable C Compiler** (also known as **pcc** or sometimes **pccm** - portable C compiler machine) is an early compiler for the C programming language written by Stephen C. Johnson of Bell Labs in the mid-1970s,[2] based in part on ideas proposed by Alan Snyder in 1973.[3] [4]

One of the first compilers that could easily be adapted to output code for different computer architectures, the compiler had a long life span. It shipped with BSD Unix until the release of 4.4BSD in 1994, when it was replaced by the GNU C Compiler. It was very influential in its day, so much so that at the beginning of the 1980s, the majority of C compilers were based on it.[5]

Features

The keys to the success of pcc were its portability and improved diagnostic capabilities. The compiler was designed so that only a few of its source files were machine-dependent. It was relatively robust to syntax errors and performed more thorough validity checks than its contemporaries.

The first C compiler, written by Dennis Ritchie, used a recursive descent parser, incorporated specific knowledge about the PDP-11, and relied on an optional machine-specific optimizer to improve the assembly language code it generated. In contrast, Johnson's pccm was based on a yacc parser generator and used a more general target machine model. Both compilers produced target-specific assembly language code which they then assembled to produce linkable object modules.

Current version

A new version of the pcc based on the original by Steve Johnson is now maintained by Anders Magnusson. The compiler is provided under the BSD licence and its development is funded by a non-profit organization called BSD Fund. According to Magnusson:

> The big benefit of it (apart from that it's BSD licensed, for license geeks) is that it is fast, 5-10 times faster than gcc, while still producing reasonable code. <...> [I]t is also quite simple to port...
>
> — Anders Magnusson[6]

This new version was added to the NetBSD pkgsrc and OpenBSD source trees in September 2007,[7] and later into the main NetBSD source tree.[8] There has been some speculation that it might eventually be used to supplant the GNU C Compiler on BSD-based operating systems,[9] though Theo de Raadt asserts that pcc is not ready yet to be a gcc replacement, and the disposal of gcc is not top priority.[10] On December 29, 2009 pcc became capable of building a functional x86 OpenBSD kernel image.[11]

pcc version 1.0 was finally released on 1 April 2011. In the announcement sent to the project donors, BSD Fund Program Manager Michael Dexter said:

> I am pleased to announce that the Portable C Compiler version 1.0 was released on April 1st, 2011 and is not an April Fools joke!

— Anders Magnusson[12]

See also

- Amsterdam Compiler Kit
- Clang
- GNU Compiler Collection
- Open Watcom

References

[1] http://pcc.ludd.ltu.se/
[2] Johnson, S.C. (1978). "A portable compiler: theory and practice" (http://doi.acm.org/10.1145/512760.512771). *Proceedings of the 5th ACM SIGACT-SIGPLAN symposium on Principles of programming languages. Tucson, Arizona.*. pp. 97–104. .
[3] Snyder, A. (1975). "A Portable Compiler for the Language C" (http://www.lcs.mit.edu/publications/specpub.php?id=717). *Master's Thesis. MIT, Cambridge, Mass.*. .
[4] Johnson, S.C. (1981). "A Tour Through the Portable C Compiler" (http://citeseer.ist.psu.edu/johnson81tour.html). *Unix Programmer's Manual, 7th edition, Volume 2*. ISBN 0-03-061743-X. .
[5] Ritchie, Dennis M. (1993). "The development of the C language" (http://plan9.bell-labs.com/who/dmr/chist.html). *The second ACM SIGPLAN conference on History of programming languages. Cambridge, Massachusetts.*. pp. 201–208. . Retrieved 2008-12-30. "At the start of the decade, nearly every compiler was based on Johnson's *pcc*; by 1985 there were many independently-produced compiler products."
[6] Erdely, Mike (2007-09-15). "BSD Licensed PCC Compiler Imported" (http://undeadly.org/cgi?action=article&sid=20070915195203&mode=expanded). *OpenBSD Journal*. . Retrieved 2011-12-17.
[7] Moerbeek, Otto (2007-09-15). "CVS: cvs.openbsd.org: src" (http://marc.info/?l=openbsd-cvs&m=118988004013923&w=2). *openbsd-cvs mailing list*. .
[8] Brownlee, David (2007-09-20). "CVS commit: src/dist/pcc" (http://mail-index.netbsd.org/source-changes/2007/09/20/0005.html). *source-changes mailing list*. .
[9] "GCC Compiler Finally Supplanted by PCC?" (http://developers.slashdot.org/article.pl?sid=07/09/17/1451239). */.*. 2007-09-17. . Retrieved 2011-12-.
[10] Matzan, Jem (2007-10-15). "More on OpenBSD's new compiler" (http://www.thejemreport.com/more-on-openbsds-new-compiler/). *The Jem Report*. . Retrieved 2011-12-17. "But that's never really been the agenda, see. Some people think we hate GNU code. But the thing is we hate large code, and buggy code that upstream does not maintain. That's the real problem... gcc gets about 5-6% slower every release, has new bugs, generates crappy code, and drives us nuts. This is just an attempt to see if something better can show up."
[11] de Weerd, Paul (2009-12-29). "Call for testing: pcc and the OpenBSD kernel" (http://undeadly.org/cgi?action=article&sid=20091228231142). *OpenBSD Journal*. . Retrieved 2011-12-17.
[12] Magnusson, Anders (2011-04-01). "1.0 Release" (http://pcc.ludd.ltu.se/1.0_release/). *Portable C Compiler*. . Retrieved 2011-12-17.

External links

- Official website (http://http://pcc.ludd.ltu.se/)

DragonFly_BSD

DragonFly BSD 2.10.1 boot loader

Company / developer	Matthew Dillon
OS family	BSD
Working state	Current
Source model	Open source
Initial release	12 July 2004
Latest stable release	3.0.2 / March 26, 2012
Available language(s)	English
Package manager	pkgsrc
Supported platforms	IA-32, x86-64
Kernel type	Hybrid
Userland	BSD
Default user interface	tcsh (root) / sh (users)
License	BSD
Preceded by	FreeBSD
Official website	www.dragonflybsd.org [1]

DragonFly BSD is a free Unix-like operating system created as a fork of FreeBSD 4.8. Matthew Dillon, an Amiga developer in the late 1980s and early 1990s and a FreeBSD developer between 1994 and 2003, began work on DragonFly BSD in June 2003 and announced it on the FreeBSD mailing lists on July 16, 2003.[2]

Dillon started DragonFly in the belief that the methods and techniques being adopted for threading and symmetric multiprocessing in FreeBSD 5[3] would lead to poor system performance and cause maintenance difficulties. He sought to correct these suspected problems within the FreeBSD project.[4] Due to ongoing conflicts with other FreeBSD developers over the implementation of his ideas[5] his ability to directly change the FreeBSD code was eventually revoked. Despite this, the DragonFly BSD and FreeBSD projects still work together contributing bug fixes, driver updates and other system improvements to each other.

Intended to be the logical continuation of the FreeBSD 4.x series, DragonFly's development has diverged significantly from FreeBSD's, including a new Light Weight Kernel Threads implementation (*LWKT*), a light weight ports/messaging system, and feature-rich HAMMER file system.[6] Many concepts planned for DragonFly were inspired by the AmigaOS operating system.[7]

System design

Kernel

Like most modern kernels, DragonFly is a hybrid, containing features of both monolithic and microkernels, such as the message passing capability of microkernels enabling larger portions of the OS to benefit from protected memory, as well as retaining the speed of monolithic kernels for certain critical tasks. The messaging subsystem being developed is similar to those found in microkernels such as Mach, though it is less complex by design. DragonFly's messaging subsystem has the ability to act in either a synchronous or asynchronous fashion, and attempts to use this capability to achieve the best performance possible in any given situation.[8]

According to developer Matthew Dillon, progress being made to provide both device input/output (I/O) and virtual file system (VFS) messaging capabilities that will enable the remainder of the project goals to be met. The new infrastructure will allow many parts of the kernel to be migrated out into userspace; here they will be more easily debugged as they will be smaller, isolated programs, instead of being small parts entwined in a larger chunk of code. Additionally, the migration of select kernel code into userspace has the benefit of making the system more robust; if a userspace driver crashes, it will not crash the kernel.[9]

System calls are being split into userland and kernel versions and being encapsulated into messages. This will help reduce the size and complexity of the kernel by moving variants of standard system calls into a userland compatibility layer, and help maintain forwards and backwards compatibility between DragonFly versions. Linux and other Unix-like OS compatibility code is being migrated out similarly. Multiple instances of the native userland compatibility layer created in jails could give DragonFly functionality similar to that found in UML, though DragonFly's virtualization does not require special drivers to communicate with the real hardware on the computer.[7]

Threading

As support for multiple processor architectures complicates symmetric multiprocessing (SMP) support,[5] DragonFly BSD limits its supported platforms to x86 and x86-64, with both single processor and SMP models.[10] Since version 1.10, DragonFly supports 1:1 userland threading (one kernel thread for every userland thread),[11] which is seen as a relatively simple and easy to maintain solution.[7] Inherited from FreeBSD, DragonFly also supports SMP multi-threading imported.[12]

In DragonFly, threads are locked to CPUs by design, and each processor has its own LWKT scheduler. Threads are never preemptively switched from one processor to another; they are only migrated by the passing of an inter-processor interrupt (IPI) message between the CPUs involved. Inter-processor thread scheduling is also accomplished by sending asynchronous IPI messages. One advantage to this clean compartmentalization of the threading subsystem is that the processors' on-board caches in Symmetric Multiprocessor Systems do not contain duplicated data, allowing for higher performance by giving each processor in the system the ability to use its own cache to store different things to work on.[7]

The *LWKT* subsystem is being employed to partition work among multiple kernel threads (for example in the networking code there is one thread per protocol per processor), reducing competition by removing the need to share certain resources among various kernel tasks.[5]

Shared resources protection

In order to run safely on multiprocessor machines, access to shared resources (like files, data structures) must be serialized so that threads or processes do not attempt to modify the same resource at the same time. In order to prevent multiple threads from accessing or modifying a shared resource simultaneously, DragonFly employs critical sections, and serializing tokens to prevent concurrent access. While both Linux and FreeBSD 5 employ fine-grained mutex models to achieve higher performance on multiprocessor systems, DragonFly does not.[5] Until recently,

DragonFly also employed spls, but these were replaced with critical sections.

Much of the system's core, including the *LWKT* subsystem, the IPI messaging subsystem and the new kernel memory allocator, are lockless, meaning that they work without using mutexes, and operate on a per-CPU basis. Critical sections are used to protect against local interrupts and operate on a per-CPU basis, guaranteeing that a thread currently being executed will not be preempted.[11]

Serializing tokens are used to prevent concurrent accesses from other CPUs and may be held simultaneously by multiple threads, ensuring that only one of those threads is running at any given time. Blocked or sleeping threads therefore do not prevent other threads from accessing the shared resource unlike a thread that is holding a mutex. Among other things, the use of serializing tokens prevents many of the situations that could result in deadlocks and priority inversions when using mutexes, as well as greatly simplifying the design and implementation of a many-step procedure that would require a resource to be shared among multiple threads. The serializing token code is evolving into something quite similar to the "Read-copy-update" feature now available in Linux. Unlike Linux's current RCU implementation, DragonFly's is being implemented such that only processors competing for the same token are affected rather than all processors in the computer.[13]

DragonFly uses a slab allocator, which requires neither mutexes nor blocking operations for memory assignment tasks and, unlike the code it replaced, is multiprocessor safe.[14] It was eventually ported to be utilized outside the kernel in a replacement to the old userland malloc implementation.[15]

Virtual kernel

Since release 1.8 DragonFly has a new virtualization mechanism similar to UML,[16] allowing to run another kernel in the userland. The virtual kernel (*vkernel*) is run in completely isolated environment with emulated network and storage interfaces, thus simplifying testing kernel subsystems and clustering features.[7] [9]

The vkernel has two important differences from the real kernel: it lacks many routines for dealing with the low-level hardware management and it uses C standard library (libc) functions in place of in-kernel implementations wherever possible. As both real and virtual kernel are compiled from the same code base, this effectively means that platform-dependent routines and re-implementations of libc functions are clearly separated in a source tree.[17]

The virtualized platform vkernel runs on is built on top of high-level abstractions provided by the real kernel. These abstractions include the kqueue-based timer, the console (mapped to the virtual terminal where vkernel is executed), the disk image and virtual kernel ethernet device (*VKE*), tunneling all packets to the host's tap interface.[18]

Package management

DragonFly previously used FreeBSD's Ports system for third party software, but since the 1.4 release, NetBSD's pkgsrc is the official package management system. With pkgsrc, the DragonFly developers are largely freed of having to maintain a large number of third party programs while still having access to up to date applications.[19] The pkgsrc developers also benefit from this arrangement as it helps to ensure the portability of the code.[4]

CARP support

The initial implementation of Common Address Redundancy Protocol (commonly referred as *CARP*) to was finished in March 2007.[20] As of 2011, CARP support is integrated into DragonFly BSD.[21]

HAMMER file system

Alongside with Unix File System, which is typically the default file system on BSDs, DragonFly BSD supports HAMMER file system. It was developed specifically for DragonFly BSD to provide a feature-rich yet better designed analogue of then increasingly popular ZFS.[7] [9] [22]

HAMMER supports configurable file system history, snapshots, checksumming, data deduplication and other features typical for file systems of its kind.[16] Though its performance is currently beyond the similar file systems like ZFS or btrfs, it is recognised as an interesting and perspective option.[23]

The next generation of HAMMER file system (*HAMMER2*) is being developed by Dillon, who stated his intent to focus on this project for the whole year 2012. As of 8 February 2012, the dedicated branch in DragonFly's source code repository was created. The earliest usable state of the file system is expected by July 2012; the final release is planned for 2013.[24] [25]

devfs

In 2007 DragonFly BSD received a new device file system (devfs), which dynamically adds and removes device nodes, allows accessing devices by connection paths, recognises drives by serial numbers and removes the need for pre-populated /dev file system hierarchy. It was implemented as a Google Summer of Code'2009 project.[26]

Application snapshots

DragonFly BSD supports Amiga-style *resident applications* feature: it takes a snapshot of a large, dynamically linked program's virtual memory space after loading, allowing future instances of the program to start much more quickly than it otherwise would have. This replaces the prelinking capability that was being worked on earlier in the project's history, as the resident support is much more efficient. Large programs like those found in KDE Software Compilation with many shared libraries will benefit the most from this support.[27]

Development and distribution

As with FreeBSD and OpenBSD, the developers of DragonFly BSD are slowly replacing K&R style C code with more modern, ANSI equivalents. Similar to other operating systems, DragonFly's version of the GNU Compiler Collection has an enhancement called the Stack-Smashing Protector (ProPolice) enabled by default, providing some additional protection against buffer overflow based attacks. It should be noted that as of 23 July 2005, the kernel is no longer built with this protection by default.[27]

Being a derivative of FreeBSD, DragonFly has inherited an easy-to-use integrated build system that can rebuild the entire base system from source with only a few commands. The DragonFly developers use the Git version control system to manage changes to the DragonFly source code. Unlike its parent FreeBSD, DragonFly has both stable and unstable releases in a single source tree, due to a smaller developer base.[5]

Like the other BSD kernels (and those of most modern operating systems), DragonFly employs a built-in kernel debugger to help the developers find kernel bugs. Furthermore, as of October 2004, a debug kernel, which makes bug reports more useful for tracking down kernel-related problems, is installed by default, at the expense of a relatively small quantity of disk space. When a new kernel is installed, the backup copy of the previous kernel and its modules are stripped of their debugging symbols to further minimize disk space usage.

Distribution media

The operating system is distributed as a Live CD and Live USB (*full X11* flavour available) that boots into a complete DragonFly system.[16] [26] It includes the base system and a complete set of manual pages, and may include source code and useful packages in future versions. The advantage of this is that with a single CD you can install the software onto a computer, use a full set of tools to repair a damaged installation, or demonstrate the capabilities of the system without installing it. Daily snapshots for both i386 and x86-64 architectures are available from the master site for those who want to install the most recent versions of DragonFly without building from source.

Like the other free open source BSDs, DragonFly is distributed under the terms of the modern version of the BSD license.

Release history

Version	Date[28]	Changes
3.0	February 22, 2012	• multiprocessor-capable kernel became the default • HAMMER performance improvements • TrueCrypt-compatible encryption support • dm-crypt replaced with compatible BSD-licensed library • enhanced POSIX compatibility • device driver for ECC memory • major network protocol stack and SMP improvements • ACPI-related improvements
2.10	April 26, 2011	• Giant lock removed from every area except the virtual memory subsystem • HAMMER deduplication • GCC 4.4 • bridging system rewritten • significant performance improvements
2.8	October 30, 2010	• Wi-Fi stack ported from FreeBSD • Logical volume management • dm-crypt • new disk scheduler • reduced giant lock usage
2.6	April 6, 2010	• swapcache • tmpfs ported from NetBSD • HAMMER and general I/O improvements
2.4	September 16, 2009	• devfs • New AHCI driver • Network File System improvements • full x86-64 support
2.2	February 17, 2009	• HAMMER officially production-ready[16] • major stability improvements • new release media: LiveDVD and LiveUSB
2.0	July 20, 2008	• major HAMMER improvements
1.12	February 26, 2008	• OpenBSD's hardware sensors framework imported from FreeBSD • Bluetooth stack • GCC 4.1 • DragonFly Mail Agent • support for the 386 CPU dropped • preliminary x86-64 support (not functional) • experimental HAMMER support

Version	Date	Features
1.10	August 6, 2007	• userland threading system • Advanced Host Controller Interface support • GUID Partition Table support
1.8	January 30, 2007	• virtual kernel implementation
1.6	July 24, 2006	• new random number generator • IEEE 802.11 framework refactored • major giant lock, clustering and userland VFS improvements • major stability improvements[29]
1.4	January 7, 2006	• GCC 3.4 • pkgsrc used by default[29] • Citrus imported from the NetBSD[30]
1.2	April 8, 2005	• TCP SACK • TCP Performance tuning • ALTQ and PF • thread-local storage • Console over IEEE 1394 • Namecache infrastructure rewritten • X11 support • pkgsrc support
1.0	July 12, 2004	• *technology showcase* • new BSD Installer • LWKT subsystem and lightweight ports/messaging system • mostly MP safe networking stack • lockless memory allocator • variant symlinks • application checkpointing support.[5]

See also

• Comparison of BSD operating systems

References

[1] http://www.dragonflybsd.org

[2] Dillon, Matthew (2003-07-16), "Announcing DragonFly BSD!" (http://lists.freebsd.org/pipermail/freebsd-current/2003-July/006889.html), *freebsd-current mailing list*, , retrieved 2007-07-26

[3] Lehey, Greg (2001) (pdf), *Improving the FreeBSD SMP implementation* (http://www.lemis.com/~grog/SMPng/USENIX/paper.pdf), USENIX, , retrieved 2012-02-22

[4] Kerner, Sean Michael (2006-01-10), "New DragonFly Released For BSD Users" (http://www.internetnews.com/dev-news/article.php/3576426), *InternetNews*, , retrieved 2011-11-20

[5] Biancuzzi, Federico (2004-07-08), "Behind DragonFly BSD" (http://www.onlamp.com/pub/a/bsd/2004/07/08/dragonfly_bsd_interview.html), *O'Reilly Media*, , retrieved 2011-11-20

[6] Loli-Queru, Eugenia (2004-03-13), "Interview with Matthew Dillon of DragonFly BSD" (http://www.osnews.com/story.php?news_id=6338), *OSNews*, , retrieved 2012-02-22

[7] Chisnall, David (2007-06-15), "DragonFly BSD: UNIX for Clusters?" (http://www.informit.com/articles/article.aspx?p=766375), *InformIT*, , retrieved 2011-11-22

[8] Hsu, Jeffery M. (pdf), *The DragonFly BSD Operating System* (http://people.freebsd.org/~hsu/papers/dragonflybsd.asiabsdcon04.pdf), , retrieved 2011-11-20

[9] Andrews, Jeremy (2007-08-06), "Interview: Matthew Dillon" (http://www.kerneltrap.org/node/14116), *KernelTrap*, archived (http://web.archive.org/web/20110515101806/http://kerneltrap.org/node/14116) from the original on 2011-05-15,

[10] "DragonFly BSD MP Performance Significantly Improved" (http://www.osnews.com/story/25334/DragonFly_BSD_MP_Performance_Significantly_Improved), *OSNews*, 2011-11-16, , retrieved 2011-11-19

[11] Luciani, Robert (2009-05-24) (pdf), *M:N threading in DragonflyBSD* (http://web.archive.org/web/20101223004617/http://www.dcbsdcon.org/speakers/slides/luciani_dcbsdcon2009.pdf), BSDCon, archived from the original (http://www.dcbsdcon.org/speakers/

slides/luciani_dcbsdcon2009.pdf) on 2010-12-23,

[12] Sherrill, Justin (2004-01-11), *Paying off already* (http://www.shiningsilence.com/dbsdlog/2004/01/11/194.html), , retrieved
       2011-11-20

[13] Pistritto, Joe; Dillon, Matthew; Sherrill, Justin C. et al. (2004-04-24), "Serializing token" (http://thread.gmane.org/gmane.os.
       dragonfly-bsd.kernel/4436), *kernel mailing list*, , retrieved 2012-03-20

[14] Bonwick, Jeff; Adams, Jonathan (2002-01-03), *Magazines and Vmem: Extending the Slab Allocator to Many CPUs and Arbitrary Resources*
       (http://www.usenix.org/event/usenix01/bonwick.html), USENIX, , retrieved 2011-11-20

[15] Dillon, Matthew (2009-04-23), "New libc malloc committed" (http://leaf.dragonflybsd.org/mailarchive/kernel/2009-04/msg00021.
       html), *kernel mailing list*, , retrieved 2011-08-08

[16] Vervloesem, Koen (2010-04-21), "DragonFly BSD 2.6: towards a free clustering operating system" (http://lwn.net/Articles/384200/),
       LWN.net, , retrieved 2011-11-19

[17] Economopoulos, Aggelos (2007-04-16), "A peek at the DragonFly Virtual Kernel" (http://lwn.net/Articles/228404/), *LWN.net* (part 1), ,
       retrieved 2011-12-08

[18] Economopoulos, Aggelos (2007-04-16), "A peek at the DragonFly Virtual Kernel" (http://lwn.net/Articles/230658/), *LWN.net* (part 2), ,
       retrieved 2011-12-08

[19] Weinem, Mark (2007), *Joerg Sonnenberger about pkgsrc on DragonFly BSD and his pkgsrc development projects.* (http://www.netbsd.
       org/gallery/10years.html#sonnenberger), "10 years of pkgsrc" (http://www.netbsd.org/gallery/10years.html), *NetBSD*, , retrieved
       2011-11-22

[20] Buschmann, Jonathan (2007-03-14), "First Patch to get CARP on Dfly" (http://leaf.dragonflybsd.org/mailarchive/kernel/2007-03/
       msg00033.html), *kernel mailing list*, , retrieved 2011-11-20

[21] "CARP(4) manual page" (http://leaf.dragonflybsd.org/cgi/web-man?command=carp§ion=4), *DragonFly On-Line Manual Pages*, ,
       retrieved 2011-11-20

[22] Dillon, Matthew (2007-10-10), "Re: HAMMER filesystem update - design document" (http://leaf.dragonflybsd.org/mailarchive/kernel/
       2007-10/msg00008.html), *kernel mailing list*, , retrieved 2011-11-20

[23] Larabel, Michael (2011-01-07), "Can DragonFlyBSD's HAMMER Compete With Btrfs, ZFS?" (http://www.phoronix.com/scan.
       php?page=article&item=dragonfly_hammer), *Phoronix*, , retrieved 2011-11-20, "HAMMER does appear to be a very interesting BSD
       file-system. It is though not quite as fast as the ZFS file-system on BSD, but this is also an original file-system to the DragonFlyBSD project
       rather than being a port from OpenSolaris. Not only is HAMMER generally faster than the common UFS file-system, but it also has a much
       greater feature-set."

[24] Dillon, Matthew (2012-02-08), "DESIGN document for HAMMER2 (08-Feb-2012 update)" (http://leaf.dragonflybsd.org/mailarchive/
       users/2012-02/msg00020.html), *users*, , retrieved 2012-02-22

[25] Dillon, Matthew (2012-02-08), "hammer2 branch in dragonfly repo created - won't be operational for 6-12 months." (http://leaf.
       dragonflybsd.org/mailarchive/users/2012-02/msg00019.html), *users mailing list*, , retrieved 2012-02-22

[26] Mr (2010-01-07), "DragonFlyBSD with Matthew Dillon" (http://cisx1.uma.maine.edu/~wbackman/bsdtalk/bsdtalk184.ogg) (ogg),
       bsdtalk, , retrieved 2011-11-20

[27] "DragonFly BSD diary" (http://www.dragonflybsd.org/diary/), *DragonFly BSD*, 2006-01-07, , retrieved 2011-11-19

[28] "DragonFly: Releases" (http://www.dragonflybsd.org/releases/), *DragonFly BSD*, , retrieved 2011-11-22

[29] Kerner, Sean Michael (2006-07-25), "DragonFly BSD 1.6 Cuts the Cord" (http://www.internetnews.com/dev-news/article.php/
       3622406), *InternetNews*, , retrieved 2011-11-20

[30] Townsend, Trent (2006-01-18), "A Quick Review of DragonFly BSD 1.4" (http://www.osnews.com/story/13352/
       A_Quick_Review_of_DragonFly_BSD_1_4), *OSNews*, , retrieved 2011-11-16

GNU_Lesser_General_Public_License

The GNU LGPLv3 logo

Author	Free Software Foundation
Version	3
Publisher	Free Software Foundation, Inc.
Published	June 29, 2007
DFSG compatible	Yes
FSF approved	Yes
OSI approved	Yes
GPL compatible	Yes
Copyleft	Yes
Linking from code with a different license	Yes

The **GNU Lesser General Public License** (formerly the **GNU Library General Public License**) or **LGPL** is a free software license published by the Free Software Foundation (FSF). It was designed as a compromise between the strong-copyleft GNU General Public License or GPL and permissive licenses such as the BSD licenses and the MIT License. The GNU Library General Public License (as the LGPL was originally named) was published in 1991, and adopted the version number 2 for parity with GPL version 2. The LGPL was revised in minor ways in the 2.1 point release, published in 1999, when it was renamed the GNU Lesser General Public License to reflect the FSF's position that not all libraries should use it. Version 3 of the LGPL was published in 2007 as a list of additional permissions applied to GPL version 3.

The LGPL places copyleft restrictions on the program governed under it but does not apply these restrictions to other software that merely link with the program. There are, however, certain other restrictions on this software.

The LGPL is primarily used for software libraries, although it is also used by some stand-alone applications, most notably Mozilla and OpenOffice.org.

Differences from the GPL

The main difference between the GPL and the LGPL is that the latter allows the work to be linked with (in the case of a library, 'used by') a non-(L)GPLed program, regardless of whether it is free software or proprietary software.[1] The non-(L)GPLed program can then be distributed under any terms if it is not a derivative work. If it is a derivative work, then the program's terms must allow for *"modification for the customer's own use and reverse engineering for debugging such modifications."* Whether a work that uses an LGPL program is a derivative work or not is a legal issue. A standalone executable that dynamically links to a library, through a .so, .dll, or similar medium, is generally accepted as not being a derivative work (as defined by the LGPL). It would fall under the definition of a "work that uses the Library". The following is an excerpt of paragraph 5 of the LGPL version 2.1:

> A program that contains no derivative of any portion of the Library, but is designed to work with the Library by being compiled or linked with it, is called a "work that uses the Library". Such a work, in isolation, is not a derivative work of the Library, and therefore falls outside the scope of this License.

Essentially, if it is a "work that uses the library", then it must be possible for the software to be linked with a newer version of the LGPL-covered program. The most commonly used method for doing so is to use "a suitable shared library mechanism for linking". Alternatively, a statically linked library is allowed if either source code or linkable object files are provided.

One feature of the LGPL is that one can convert any LGPLed piece of software into a GPLed piece of software (section 3 of the license). This feature is useful for direct reuse of LGPLed code in GPLed libraries and applications, or if one wants to create a version of the code that cannot be used in proprietary software products.

Choosing to license a library under the GPL or the LGPL

The former name of "GNU Library General Public License" gave some people the impression that the FSF endorsed that libraries use the LGPL and that programs use the GPL. In February 1999, Richard Stallman wrote the essay *Why you shouldn't use the Lesser GPL for your next library* explaining that the LGPL has not been deprecated, but that one should not *necessarily* use the LGPL for all libraries:

> Which license is best for a given library is a matter of strategy... Using the ordinary GPL for a library gives free software developers an advantage over proprietary developers: a library that they can use, while proprietary developers cannot use it... When a free library's features are readily available for proprietary software through other alternative libraries... the library cannot give free software any particular advantage, so it is better to use the Lesser GPL for that library.[1]

Indeed, Stallman and the FSF sometimes advocate licenses even less restrictive than the LGPL as a matter of strategy. A prominent example was Stallman's endorsement of the use of a BSD-style license by the Vorbis project for use in its libraries.[2]

Programming languages specificity

The license uses terminology which is mainly intended for applications written in the C programming language or its family. Franz Inc. published its own preamble to the license to clarify terminology in the Lisp context. LGPL with this preamble is sometimes referred as LLGPL.[3]

In addition, Ada has a special feature, generics, that may use the MGPL license.

LGPL regarding class inheritance

Some concern has risen about the suitability of object-oriented classes in LGPL'd software being inherited by non-(L)GPL code. Clarification is given on the official GNU website:

> The LGPL contains no special provisions for inheritance, because none are needed. Inheritance creates derivative works in the same way as traditional linking, and the LGPL permits this type of derivative work in the same way as it permits ordinary function calls.[4]

See also

- Affero General Public License
- Free Software licensing
- GNU Free Documentation License
- GNU General Public License
- GNAT Modified General Public License
- GPL linking exception

References

[1] Stallman, Richard. Why you shouldn't use the Lesser GPL for your next library (http://www.fsf.org/licensing/licenses/why-not-lgpl. html). Free Software Foundation official website.

[2] Stallman, Richard. Re: [open-source] [Fwd: [icecast-dev] Xiph.org announces Vorbis Beta 4 and the Xiph.org (http://lwn.net/2001/0301/ a/rms-ov-license.php3)

[3] Preamble to the Gnu Lesser General Public License (http://opensource.franz.com/preamble.html)

[4] Turner, David. The LGPL and Java (http://www.gnu.org/licenses/lgpl-java.html). GNU official website.

External links

- LGPL Official Page (http://www.gnu.org/copyleft/lesser.html)
- Derivative Works (http://www.linuxjournal.com/article/6366)

Article Sources and Contributors

MidnightBSD *Source*: http://en.wikipedia.org/w/index.php?title=MidnightBSD *Contributors*: CRGreathouse, Edward, Frap, Hbent, Laffer1, Parsreason, Sligocki, SourSquirrel, Tedickey, Toussaint, 13 anonymous edits

Unix-like *Source*: http://en.wikipedia.org/w/index.php?title=Unix-like *Contributors*: 16@r, Acerperi, Adamantios, AdrianTM, Agarvin, Ahunt, Aladdin Sane, Aldie, AlistairMcMillan, Allens, Andrew1718, Andy16666, Angela, Athantor, BarkingFish, Bdesham, Beno1000, Betterworld, BiT, Borgx, Camje lemon, Chealer, Cheyinka, Chowbok, Chris Q, ChrisBrown, Cleared as filed, Clemwang, ColdShine, Conversion script, Crispmuncher, CyberSkull, Cybercobra, Cyclonius, Damian Yerrick, Darrien, David Gerard, Demi, Dereckson, Derek Ross, Druiloor, Dwheeler, Dylan Lake, Eequor, ElBenevolente, Ems2, EqualRights, Eraserhead1, Escape Orbit, Evice, Evil Monkey, Fibonacci, Frigoris, Funkysapien, Furrykef, GandalfDaGraay, Gareth Owen, Geronimooo, Ghettoblaster, Gogo Dodo, Grandscribe, Greenrd, Gronky, Gubbubu, Guy Harris, Haikupoet, Hans Dunkelberg, Henry W. Schmitt, Hroðulf, IJohnMac, IMSoP, Imroy, JLaTondre, JYOuyang, James Foster, Janizary, Jerryobject, Joeinwap, Joffeloff, Jonny6910, Jordandanford, JorgePeixoto, Jpp, Julesd, Juliancolton, Karnesky, Ken Arromdee, Koffieyahoo, Kulokk, Kwertii, Kychot, La Pianista, Letdorf, Limewolf, Lost.goblin, LukeyBoy, MarXidad, Marathonmike, Markpeak, Mebden, Merphant, Michael B. Trausch, Mindmatrix, Mms, Monedula, Mysekurity, N5iln, Naddy, NapoliRoma, NawlinWiki, Ni.cero, NicM, Nickj, Ossguy, Owain, Pelago, Phobos11, Pmlineditor, Polluks, Powwradota, Prolinesurfer, Psychonaut, Public Menace, Quasipalm, R'n'B, RJaguar3, Rchandra, Reisio, Revolus, Robertmh, Rvalles, SF007, Schily, Scott Ritchie, Scott Wilson, Seitz, Seth Nimbosa, Siroxo, Sligocki, Smazzin, SteinbDJ, SteveSims, Stevertigo, Taak, Tarquin, Techsmith, Teemu Leisti, Thumperward, Timir2, Tobias Bergemann, Topbanana, Trialsanderrors, Tverbeek, Tyomitch, Utcursch, Vicki Rosenzweig, Wareh, WarthogDemon, Wereon, Wernher, Whayworth, XTaran, Yes-minister, Yworo, Zvn, Öncel Acar, 217 anonymous edits

Operating_system *Source*: http://en.wikipedia.org/w/index.php?title=Operating_system *Contributors*: 10metreh, 12.245.75.xxx, 1297, 130.64.31.xxx, 149AFK, 151.30.199.xxx, 1execl, 1yesfan, 216.150.138.xxx, 28421u2232nfenfcenc, 2D, 2nth0nyj, 62.253.64.xxx, 789455dot38, 9258fahsflkh917fas, 9marksparks9, =Josh.Harris, A876, APH, AR bd, AVRS, AVand, Aaron north, Aaronstj, Abhik0904, Ablewisuk, Ablonus, Acerperi, Achowat, Adair2324, Adams kevin, Addshore, Adityachodya, AdjustShift, Adriaan, Ae-a, Afed, After Midnight, Agentlame, Ahoerstemeier, Ahunt, Ahy1, Aim Here, Aitias, Aladdin Sane, Alanbrowne, Alansohn, Alasdair, Ale jrb, AlefZet, Alegoo92, Alenaross07, AlexDitto, Alexei-ALXM, Alexf, Alexius08, Alexswilliams, Alextyhy, Alexwcovington, Alisha.4m, AlistairMcMillan, Alksentrs, Alll, Alsandro, Altay437, Alten, Althepal, Am088, Amicon, Amillar, Amphlett7, Anaxial, Andre Engels, Andrew Maiman, Andrewpmk, Android Mouse, Andy pyro, Andy16666, Andyzweb, Ang3lboy2001, Anna Lincoln, AnnaFrance, AnonMoos, Anouymous, Ansumang, Antandrus, Antonielly, Antonio Lopez, Applechair, Arakunem, Aranea Mortem, Arch dude, Archanamiya, Archer3, Ark, Arman Cagle, Aruton, Ashikpa, Ashish Gaikwad, Ashleypurdy, Astral, Atlant, Atomician, Attitude2000, Avenged Eightfold, Awaterl, Ayla, BMF81, Bachinchi, Bact, Badhaker, Badriram, Baron1984, Baronnet, Bastique, Bbbl67, Bbuss, Beland, Ben Webber, BenAveling, Bencherlite, Benneman, Beno1000, Betacommand, Bevo, Bhu z Crecelu, BiT, Bidgee, Big Brother 1984, BigDunc, Bigdumbdinosaur, Bijesh nair, BjörnBergman, Blainster, Bleh999, Blu Aardvark III, Bluemask, Bobo192, Boing! said Zebedee, Bonadea, Bongwarrior, Bookinvestor, Bornslippy, Branddobbe, Brianga, Brion VIBBER, Brolin Empey, Brownga, Bsadowski1, Btate, Bubba hotep, Buonoj, Burkeaj, Bwildasi, Cactus.man, Caknuck, Calabe1992, Callmejosh, Calltech, CalumH93, Camilo Sanchez, Caminoix, Can You Prove That You're Human, Can't sleep, clown will eat me, CanadianLinuxUser, Canageek, CanisRufus, Canterbury Tail, Capricorn42, Captain Goggles, Captain-n00dle, CarbonUnit, CarbonX, CardinalDan, Carlosvigopaz, Cartread, Casull, Cdills, Celebere, CesarB, Cfallin, Chairman S., Chaitanya.lala, Chamal N, ChaoticHeavens, Charles Nguyen, Charles dye, CharlotteWebb, Chase@osdev.org, Chatul, Chikoosahu, Chris1219, Chrisch, ChrisK02, Christian List, Christian75, Ck lostsword, Cleduc, Clindhartsen, Cllnk, Closedmouth, Clsin, Cncxbox, Cobi, Coffee, CommonsDelinker, Comperr, Conan, Conti, Conversion script, Cookdn, Coolcaesar, CoolingGibbon, Corpx, Courcelles, Cpl11, Cpiral, Cps274203, Cpuwhiz11, Crazycomputers, Create g77, Creativename, Credema, Creidieki, Cul22dude, Cuvtixo, Cybercobra, Cybiko123, CyborgTosser, D, D6, DARTH SIDIOUS 2, DBishop1984, DJ Craig, DStoykov, DVdm, Daesotho, Damian Yerrick, Dan100, DanDoughty, Daniel C, Danieltobey, Dantheman88, Darkwind, Darth Panda, Dasnov, Daverocks, David Santos, DavidCary, DavidHalko, Davidam, Davidm617617, Dawnseeker2000, DeDroa, DeadEyeArrow, Deagle AP, Debloper, Deconstructhis, Defender of torch, Dekard, Dekisugi, Delinka, Demiurge, Demonkoryu, Denisarona, Deon, DerHexer, Desolator12, DestroyerPC, Dexter Nextnumber, Dhardik007, DiaNoCHe, DigitallyBorn, Dirkbb, DirkvdM, Discospinster, Dispenser, DivineAlpha, Djonesuk, Djsasso, Dmerrill, Dmlandfair, Doh5678, Donhoraldo, Dori, Dosman, Download, Doyley, DrDnar, DreamFieldArts, Drmies, Drummondjacob, Dsda, Dudboi, Duke56, DuncanHill, Dvn805, Dyl, Dynaflow, Dysprosia, Dzubint, E Wing, E.mammadli, ERcheck, ESkog, Eab28, Easwarno1, Echo95, EconoPhysicist, EdEColbert, Edivorce, Edward, Edwy, Eeekster, Ehheh, El C, Eleete, Elkman, Ellmist, Elockid, Elsendero, Elvenmuse, Ems2, Emurphy42, Emwave, Emx, Endothermic, Enigmar007, Enna59, Enno, Ente75, Enviroboy, Epbr123, Erickanner, Erkan Yilmaz, ErkinBatu, Escape Orbit, Ethan.hardman, Ethanhardman3, EurekaLott, Eurleif, Evercat, EwokiWiki, Excirial, Eyreland, Face, Falcon Kirtaran, Falcon8765, Favonian, Feedintm, Felyza, Ferrenrock, Fish and karate, Flewis, Flonase, Florian Blaschke, Flubbit, Fobenavi, Foot, ForrestVoight, Fram, Francis2795, Frankdushantha, Frap, Fred Gandt, FredStrauss, Fredrik, Freyr, Friecode, Fronx, Fsiler, Fubar Obfusco, Furrykef, Fvasconcellos, Fyver528, GB fan, GRAHAMUK, Gail, Gaius Cornelius, Gardar Rurak, Garlovel, Gaurav1146, Gauravdce07, Gazpacho, Gbeeker, Geekman314, GeneralChrisV, Georgia guy, Geph, Gepotto, Gerard Czadowski, Ghakko, Ghettoblaster, Ghyll, Giftlite, Glacialfox, Glen, Gogo Dodo, Gogodidi, Golfington, Golftheman, GoneAwayNowAndRetired, Goodnightmush, GorillaWarfare, Gorrister, Gortu, Grafen, Graham87, Grandscribe, GrayFullbuster, Greensburger, GrooveDog, Grosscha, Ground Zero, Grover cleveland, Grunt, Gschizas, Gscshoyru, Gtgray1948, Guess Who, Gumbos, Gurch, Guy Harris, HDrake, Hammersoft, Hanii Puppy, Hannes Hirzel, Hansfn, Harry, Harryboyles, Hashar, Hawaiian717, Hdante, HebrewHammerTime, Hazard-SJ, Hdante, Heron, HexaChord, Hillel, Hirzel, Hmains, Holden15, Hqb, Hrundi Bakshi, Htaccess, Huszone, Hut 8.5, Hydrogen Iodide, II MusLiM HyBRiD II, IMSoP, Iamunknown, Ian Dunster, Ian Pitchford, Ian.thomson, Icefirearceus, Ida Shaw, Ideogram, Idleguy, Ilmari Karonen, Indon, Inferno, Lord of Penguins, Ino5hiro, Insanity Incarnate, Integralexplora, Intgr, Ioeth, Iridescent, IronGargoyle, Ishanjand, Iswariya.r, It Is Me Here, ItsMeowAnywhere, Ixfd64, J Milburn, J.delanoy, J00tel, JForget, JHunterJ, JLaTondre, JSpudeman, Jaan513, Jackfork, Jackmiles2006, James pic, JamesAM, JamesBWatson, Janitor Starr, Jarble, Jasper Deng, Jatkins, Javierito92, Jaxl, Jaysweet, Jbarta, Jclemens, Jdm64, Jdrowlands, Jebus989, Jedikaiti, Jeff G., Jeffwang, Jeltz, JeremyA, Jerome Charles Potts, Jeronimo, Jerry, Jerryobject, Jerrysmp, Jesse V., JetBlast, Jfg284, Jfmantis, Jhh51681, Jhonsrid, Jijojohnpj, Jim1138, JimPlamondon, Jimmi Hugh, Jjk, Jjupiter100, Jkl4201, JoanneB, Jobrad, JoeSmack, Joecoolatjunkmaildotcom, Joemaza, Joffeloff, John Nevard, Johnnaylor, Johnny039, Johnuniq, JonHarder, Jonathan Hall, Jordi Burguet Castell, Jorge.guillen, JorgePeixoto, Josef.94, Josepsbd, Josh the Nerd, Joshlk, Joshua Gyamfi, Joy, Jpeeling, Jstirling, Jsysinc, Julepalme, Jumbuck, Jusdafax, K7jeb, KAtremer, KDesk, KGasso, Ka Faraq Gatri, Kagredon, Kajasudhakarababu, Kamanleodickson, Karabulutis252, Karimarie, Karnesky, Karol Langner, Karolinski, Kashmiri, Katalaveno, Kathleen.wright5, Katieh5584, Kaustubh.singh, Kaypoh, Kbdank71, Kbrose, Kcordina, Ke5crz, KenBest, Kenny sh, KenshinWithNoise, Kenyon, Kerowhack, Kev19, Kevin586, Kgoetz, Khoikhoi, Kidde, Kim Bruning, Kimdino, Kjaleshire, Kjetil r, Kjkolb, Kku, Klungel, Knokej, Knownot, Kokamomi, Kotiwalo, KrakatoaKatie, Krauss, Kubanczyk, Kuru, Kushalbiswas777, Kusma, Kusunose, Kwiki, Kyle1278, Kyng, Kyuuseishu, L Kensington, LFaraone, La Pianista, Lambiam, Landroo, Latka, Law, Leaflord, LeaveSleaves, Lejarrag, LeoNomis, Letdorf, Leuko, Lifemaestro, Lightedbulb, Lindert, Linkspamremover, Linnell, Littlegeisha, Livajo, Lkatkinsmith, Lmmaaaoooo, Loadmaster, Logan, Logixoul, Lordmarlineo, Lost.goblin, Love manjeet kumar singh, Lovelac7, Lowellian, Lradrama, Lt monu, Ltomuta, Lucid, Lucy-seline, Lucyin, Luk, Lumos3, Luna Santin, Lvken7, Lysander89, Lyt701, M.r santosh kumar., M2Ys4U, M4gnum0n, MBisanz, MC MasterChef, MER-C, MONGO, Mabdul, Macintosh User, Macintosh123, Magnus Manske, Maitchy, Makeemlighter, Manassehkatz, Mandarax, Manickam001, Manmohan Brahma, Manojbp07, Manticore, March23.1999, Marek69, MarioRadev, MarkSG, Markaci, Marko75, MarmotteNZ, Martarius, Martin smith 637, Martinwguy, Masonkinyon, Materialscientist, MattGiuca, Mattbr, Matthardingu, Matthuxtable, MattieTK, Mav, Max Naylor, Maxim, Maximus Rex, Maziotis, Mbalamuruga, Mblumber, Mc hammerutime, McDutchie, McLovin34, Mcloud91, Mdd, Mdikici, Meaghan, Medovina, Meegs, Melab-1, Melsaran, Memset, Mendalus, Meneth, Meowmeow8956, Merlion444, MetaEntropy, Miaers, Michael B. Trausch, MichaelR., Michaelas10, Mickyfitz13, Mike33, Mike92591, MikeLynch, Mikeblas, Milan Keršláger, Mild Bill Hiccup, Minesweeper, Minghong, Miquonranger03, Mirror Vax, Miss Madeline, MisterCharlie, Mistman123, MithrandirAgain, Mmxx, Mnemoc, Mononomic, Monz, Moondyne, Mortus Est, MovGP0, Mppl3z, Mptb3, Mr.Z-man, MrOllie, MrPaul84, Mrankur, Mthomp1998, Muehlburger, Mufka, Mujz1, Muralihbh, Murderbike, Musiphil, Mwanner, Mwheatland, Mwtoews, Mxn, Müslimix, N sharma000, N419BH, N5iln, NNLauron, Nakon, Nanshu, Naohiro19 revertvandal, NapoliRoma, Nasnema, NawlinWiki, Nayak143, Nayvik, Ndavidow, NellieBly, Nergaal, Neversay.misher, Ngch89, Ngien, Ngyikp, Nick, Nikai, Ninuxpdb, Nixeagle, Njuuton, Nk, Nlu, No Guru, Nobody Ent, Noldoaran, Nono64, Norm, Northamerica1000, NotAnonymous0, Nothingisoftensomething, Notinasnaid, Nrabinowitz, Nsaa, Numlockfishy, Nvt, Nwusr123log, O.Koslowski, OKtosiTe, Ocolon, Oda Mari, Odell421, Odie5533, Ohnoitsjamie, Olathe, Oliverdl, Olivier, OllieWilliamson, Olurotimi0, Omicronpersei8, Omniplex, Ondertitel, Onorem, Oosoom, Optimisticrizan, OrgasGirl, Orrs, Oxymoron83, P.Marlow, Papadopa, Parasti, Patato, Patrick, Paul E T, Paul1337, Pcbsder, Pepper, PeterStJohn, Petrb, PhJ, PhantomS, Phgao, Phil websurfer@yahoo.com, Philip Howard, Philip Trueman, Photonik UK, Piano non troppo, Pierre Monteux, Pinethicket, Pinkadelica, Pithree, Plasticup, PlutosGeek, Pmlineditor, Polluks, Polyamorph, Pontiacsunfire08, Posix memalign, Prashanthomesh, PrestonH, Programming geek, Prolog, Prophile, Pruefer, Public Menace, Puffin, Qaanol, Quarkuar, Qwerty0, Qwyrxian, R'n'B, R. S. Shaw, RA0808, RB972, RTC, Raanoo, Rabi Javed, Raffaele Megabyte, RainbowOfLight, Rainsak, Rami R, Ramif 47, Random Hippopotamus, RandomAct, RaseaC, Ratnadeepm, RattusMaximus, RavenXtra, Rayngwf, Raysonho, Raywil, RazorICE, Rbakels, Rbanzai, Rdsmith4, Reach Out to the Truth, RedWolf, Reedy, Rektide, Remixsoft10, Rettetast, RexNL, Rfc1394, Rhyswynne, Riana, Rich Farmbrough, Rilak, Rjgarr, Rjwilmsi, Rlinfinity, Rmere, Rmhermen, Robert K S, Robert Merkel, RobertG, Robertwharvey, RockMaster, Rockstone35, Rodri316, RogierBrussee, Rokfaith, Rolandg, Romanm, Ronark, Ronhjones, RossPatterson, Rotem Dan, RoyBoy, Rrelf, Rror, Rubena, Rubicon, Rzelnik, S.borchers, S10462, SF007, SNIyer12, SPQRobin, Safinaskar, Sainath468, Sakariyerirash, Sam Vimes, SampigeVenkatesh, Sander123, Sanfranman59, Sango123, Sardanaphalus, Sarikaanand, Scherr, SchmuckyTheCat, SchuminWeb, Schwallex, Schzmo, Sdfisher, Sean William, Seba5618, Sedmic, Senator Palpatine, Sewing, Shadowjams, Sharanbngr, Sharkert, SheikYerBooty, Shizhao, Shreevatsa, Shreshth91, Shriram, Sidious1741, Sigma 7, Signalhead, Silas S. Brown, Simon the Dragon, SimonP, Simxp, Sir Nicholas de Mimsy-Porpington, SirGrant, SirGre, SivaKumar, Skarebo, Skomes, Slgrandson, Slogan621, Slon02, SmackEater, Smadge1, Snowmanradio, Snowolf, Socalaaron, Socrates2008, SocratesJedi, SolKarma, SolarisBigot, Sommers, Sophus Bie, South Bay, Sp, Spanglegluppet, Sparkle24, SpooK, SpuriousQ, Squash, Sridip, Staffwaterboy, Stealthmartin, Stephen Gilbert, Stephen Turner, Stephenb, Stephenchou0722, SteveSims, Stevenj, Stewartadcock, Stickee, Stormie, SudoGhost, SunCountryGuy01, SunCreator, Sunay419, Super Mac Gamer, SuperLuigi31, Superswade, SusanLesch, Susheel verma, Sven Manguard, Sven nestle, Sweet blueberry pie, Synchronism, Syzygy, THEN WHO WAS PHONE?, THeReDragOn, Ta bu shi da yu, Tannin, TarkusAB, Tarmo Tanilsoo, Tarquin, Tasting boob, Tatrgel, Tdrtdr, Tdscanuck, TempestSA, TexasAndroid, Texture, Tgeairn, Tgnome, The Anome, The Random Editor, The Thing That Should Not Be, The undertow, The1DB, TheAMmollusc, TheNewPhobia, TheWorld, Thecomputist, Theda, Thedjatclubrock, TheguX, Themoose8, Theshibboleth, Thingg, Thorpe, Thumperward, Tide rolls, TigerShark, Timir Saxa, Titoxd, Tnxman307, Tobias Bergemann, Toddst1, Tokai, Tom Hek, Tom harrison, Tomcool, Tommy2010, TommyB7973, Tompsci, Tony1, Tothwolf, Touch Of Light, Tpbradbury, Tpk5010, Traroth, Travelbird, Trevj, Trevjs, Trimaine, Triona, Trisweb, Triwbe, TurboForce, Twas Now, Twistedkevin, Twitty666, Twsx, Tyler, Tyomitch, Typhoon, Tyrel, Ultimus, Umofomia, Unbreakable MJ, Uncle Dick, Unixguy, Unknown-xyz, Uogl, Upthegro, Ursu17, Urvashi.iyogi, Useight, User A1, Utahraptor ostrommaysi, Utilitytrack, VampWillow, Vanessaezekowitz, Vanished user 39948282, Vbigdeli, VegaDark, Verrai, Vicenarian, Vikrant manore, Vincenzo.romano, Viriditas, Vorosgy, Vox Humana 8',

Vrenator, W163, WJetChao, Wapcaplet, Wareh, Warren, Warut, Wasted Sapience, Waterjuice, Wavelength, Wayward, Wbm1058, Wdfarmer, Wdflake, Weedwhacker128, WellHowdyDoo, White Shadows, Who.was.phone, Widefox, WikHead, Wiki Wikardo, Wiki alf, WikiDan61, WikiPuppies, WikiTome, Wikievil666, Wikiloop, Wikipelli, WilyD, Winchelsea, Wingnutamj, Winhunter, Winston365, Wisconsinsurfer, Wk muriithi, Wknight94, Wluka, Woohookitty, World-os.com, WorldBrains, Wormsgoat, Wtmitchell, Wtshymanski, Wwagner, X42bn6, Xdenizen, Yaronf, Yellowdesk, Yes-minister, Yidisheryid, Yoink23, Youwillnevergetthis, Yunshui, Yworo, Zephyrus67, Zfr, Zidonuke, Zigger, Ziiike, Zlemming, Zondor, Zotel, Zx-man, Zzuuzz, 212, Ævar Arnfjörð Bjarmason, Милан Јелисавчић, سارای نورون‌, ಇಷ್ಟ ಮಾಡಿಕೊ, , 3140 anonymous edits

FreeBSD Source: http://en.wikipedia.org/w/index.php?title=FreeBSD Contributors: 130.64.31.xxx, A-giau, Acerperi, AdrianChadd, AgadaUrbanit, Ahoerstemeier, Alansohn, AlastairIrvine, Ales-76, AlistairMcMillan, Allen Moore, AllenM, Alliance1911, Almaliq, Altenmann, Ancheta Wis, Angrykeyboarder, ArabChat, Arch dude, Armanx64, Arved, Asapilu, Ashawley, Astrolox, Astudent, Authtech, Avstin, B0o-supermario, Badboyjamie, Bawolff, Bender235, Beno1000, Boarder8925, Borgx, Bovineone, Bsdlogical, Bugnot, CRGreathouse, Cacuija, Cadsuane Melaidhrin, Calvino, CanisRufus, Captain panda, Cekli829, Chargh, Chealer, Chris the speller, Christian List, Christopher Forster, Ciao 90, Cjthellama, Clockwork Soul, Committar, CommonsDelinker, Coneslayer, Conversion script, Cooperised, Cougars, Crakkpot, Creidieki, Crucis, CyberSkull, Cybercobra, Cyril, Czeror, DC-10 rocks, DCEvoCE, DagErlingSmørgrav, Darrien, DarwinPeacock, David Gerard, Debackerl, Debresser, Dennylin93, DerekMorr, Devin lapach, Dinjiin, DocWatson42, Doktor Who, Don Reba, Dori, Douglas Ray, Doze, Dreamertan, Drilnoth, Driv3r, Drj, Dustin gayler, Dysprosia, E-user, EIFY, EWayte, Echimu, EdBever, Edward, Electron9, Ems2, Endx7, Equaaldoors, Eraserhead1, Erik-the-red, Etaon, Evercat, Evice, Evil Monkey, Fanf, Farrokhi, Fbs greenglow, Feezo, Fender0107401, Ferritecore, Fjarlq, Flata, Fleminra, FlorentThoumie, Fostermarkd, Fpga, Freakofnurture, Fsiler, Fubar Obfusco, Fultus, Fvw, GL9!, GM Ghost, Gadago, Gaius Cornelius, Gareth McCaughan, Garyjh512, Gatta, Gavinatkinson, Ghettoblaster, Gigglesworth, Gludwiczak, Gnulinux, Goatasaur, Gobonobo, Gogo Dodo, Gogobera, Graue, Green caterpillar, Greenman, Gronky, Groogle, Gruime, Gudeldar, Guyjohnston, Gwen Gale, Gwern, Haakon, Hadas583, Half price, Hansivers, Hashar, Henriknj, Heramball, Hn, Homer Landskirty, Horst.Burkhardt, HunterX, Hux, Hydrargyrum, ISEETRUTH, IanOsgood, Ida Shaw, Ikon16, IlariS, Iliev, InTheCastle, Infofarmer, Intgr, InverseHypercube, Isilanes, Ivoras, Jacob Myers, James.pole, Janizary, Jbramley, Jcrook1987, Jeffb0, Jiang, Jimsve, Jlehen, Jlenthe, JohnOwens, Jonabbey, JorgePeixoto, Joseph Koshy, Joy, Jquindlen, Jtalledo, Jtgerman, Julianbrelsford, Jvhertum, Jóna Þórunn, K1, K3rb, Kace7, Kate, Kbrose, Kenyon, Keramida, Kl4m-AWB, Knelp, Komap, Koolabsol, Kraenar, Krellis, Kronos, Kyng, Latiligence, Lavajoe, Lee Carre, Legios, Letdorf, Lexlex, LocoBurger, Locos epraix, Logixoul, Lotje, Lupin, Lwhsu, M gol, M1ss1ontomars2k4, MJA, MK8, MZMcBride, MagV, Magister Mathematicae, Makemi, MarkusHagenlocher, Marudubshinki, Massic80, Mastotosugiarto, Mav, Max Gesler, Maxis ftw, Mboverload, Mehmetk, Melancholie, Mendalus, Michael B. Trausch, Michael iedema, Mike92591, Mindmatrix, Mipadi, Mixx941, Mmmready, Moink, Monoecus, Morton.lin, Msreeharsha, MureninC, Mux, Mwtoews, Mww42, Mxn, Mysidia, Nackpere, Naddy, Nanshu, NapoliRoma, Nave.notnilc, Neilc, Net65536, Netmaskx90, NicM, Oberst, Obscuranym, Octahedron80, Olathe, Palica, Parklandspanaway, Parsreason, Pauli133, Pbrezny, Pcarter7, Pelister, Pengo, PeterJeremy, Peyre, Pgan002, Piet Delport, Pile0nades, Pinged007, Pinikas, Pmc, Pol098, Ptitgnu, Ptomes, PuerExMachina, Python eggs, Qiaoyang, Quamsta, Quietust, Qutezuce, Qwitchibo, Raul654, Raysonho, Rbeef, Rbuj, Rdivacky, RedWolf, Redjar, RedxelaSinnak, Reisio, RenamedUser2, Rich Farmbrough, RichardTector, Richardcavell, RickK, Rjwilmsi, Rlmorgan, Robertmh, Romx, S.Örvarr.S, SCARECROW, SF007, Saint-billy, Saper, Saucepan, Sav vas, Scott1andrews, Scotw, Shne, Simfan147, Singleton2000, Sirmikester, Slashme, Sliders, Sligocki, Snaxe920, Somebody in the WWW, SpaceRocket, SpeedyGonsales, Sperling, SpigotMap, Splash, Squash, Srinivas2, Staalmannen, Ste4k, Stevertigo, Stewartadcock, Storkk, Strbenjr, Stront ox, StuffOfInterest, Suruena, Sv23, Sweetness46, Syph, Taxman, Technodo, Tedickey, Telonir, The Divine Fluffalizer, TheSolomon, TheWishy, Thewalrus, ThierryVignaud, ThomasHarte, Thorenn, Thumperward, Tide rolls, TimBentley, Tmopkisn, Tothwolf, Toussaint, Trasz, TruckMonkey, Tyomitch, Uncle G, Unyoyega, Up23, VAcharon, VShaka, Vanieter, Vedantabarooah, Victor, Victortc, Virtual bob, Vrkaul, Warut, Wernher, Wickedy, Wik, Wilbern Cobb, Williamanthony, XTaran, Yekrats, Yurivict, Zade Khalyym, Zak.l, Zedisn, Zeno Gantner, Zensufi, Zfr, Zollerriia, Zxombie, Ævar Arnfjörð Bjarmason, Милан Јелисавчић, 737 anonymous edits

PC-BSD Source: http://en.wikipedia.org/w/index.php?title=PC-BSD Contributors: Aardvark92, Abhikohli, Afroman10496, Alisha.4m, Amux, Badon, Bforte, Biffthemonkey, Blackaddoer, Blaxthos, Boarder8925, CRGreathouse, Chimin 07, Christopher Forster, Dannyb13, Derbeth, DesbWit, Dnstest, Drange net, ESkog, Electron9, Ergo4sum, Evice, FatalError, Frap, Freedomlinux, Gnulinux, Gnuslov, Gronky, Guy Harris, Gwen Gale, Gwern, Hidro, Hoo man, Itsmine, Jeshan, JoeSmack, Joy, Jtalledo, Kace7, Kl4m-AWB, Klpowell, Kmf, Kyng, Lavenderbunny, Libertyernie2, Lightmouse, LimoWreck, Lkt1126, Locos epraix, MRqtH2, MagV, Mark alfred, MarkusHagenlocher, Melancholie, Mindmatrix, Nachi, Necro86, Niels Olson, Nr10232, Oskar Sigvardsson, Parsreason, PaulRg, Paxcoder, Pipedreamergrey, Raphael Frey, Rbuj, RenamedUser2, Rinick, Rjwilmsi, Rwwww, SF007, Samsara, Sandman q23, Say nesh, Secretlondon, Sether, Sharru Kinnu III, Sims2789, Sixteen Left, Soimort, Someoneinmyheadbutit'snotme, Somethings90, SpaceRocket, Stassats, Suwatest, Techie2, Techtonik, Tedickey, TheRingess, Tigga en, Timothy.arthur, Typhoon, Vivin, Wildnox, 164 anonymous edits

DesktopBSD Source: http://en.wikipedia.org/w/index.php?title=DesktopBSD Contributors: Alisha.4m, Amberroom, CRGreathouse, Carnildo, Csl77, DarkElf109, Derbeth, Destin, Feedmecereal, Gnulinux, Gronky, Guy Harris, Gwen Gale, Gwern, Hammertime2009, Icedog, Jtalledo, Kl4m-AWB, Kronos, Lucifer Spam, MagV, MelbourneStar, Mindmatrix, Mysidia, Nikkimaria, Parsreason, RenamedUser2, Sether, Shooke, SilverFox, Suwatest, Tchannon, Techstepp, Tedickey, Typhoner, Typhoon, ViperSnake151, 68 anonymous edits

GNUstep Source: http://en.wikipedia.org/w/index.php?title=GNUstep Contributors: Akanemoto, Aldaniel, Andre Engels, Ant, Arturus, Bdesham, Bheron, BjKa, Brettz9, CYD, Cglue, Chealer, Ctachme, David Gerard, DenisKrivosheev, Dysprosia, Edward, Frap, Gioto, Gronky, Gürkan Sengün, IOOI, Imz, JBsupreme, Jerome Charles Potts, Jerryobject, Jhf, Jonas August, KAMiKAZOW, Karam.Anthony.K, Kbdank71, Kiplingw, Kl4m-AWB, Kmk75s, Kricxjo, Krischik, Leoadec, Liebeskind, LittleDan, Lupin, MarkusHagenlocher, Mike Schwartz, Mipadi, Multix, Nixdorf, Norm, Ojw, Pinkmanlovemouth, Pnm, Rfl, Screwjack, Siroxo, Sjorford, Stefan Urbanek, SymlynX, TMC1221, ThomasHarte, Thumperward, Tim1357, Toussaint, Tullius, Unforgettableid, Warren, Where, Whitebox, Wiki Wikardo, Yworo, Ævar Arnfjörð Bjarmason, 68 anonymous edits

Release_engineering Source: http://en.wikipedia.org/w/index.php?title=Release_engineering Contributors: 041744, AGK, Abhinavvaid, Andreas Kaufmann, Anvish, Dagg, Daniel.Cardenas, Freshbaked, Furrykef, Gwhodgson, Hashar, Imeshev, JCrenshaw, JonHarder, Jwarhol, Lightblade, LilHelpa, Longhair, Lycurgus, Mdd, Mikeblas, Milkfish, N-miyo, NuclearWinner, Sardanaphalus, Sivala, Stevage, Tedickey, Tracyragan, Wolfdancer, 31 anonymous edits

Portable_C_Compiler Source: http://en.wikipedia.org/w/index.php?title=Portable_C_Compiler Contributors: 7265, AlistairMcMillan, AnonMoos, Bobnorwal, Bolwerk, Cmgross, Czarkoff, DAGwyn, Eschnett, Frap, Gavinatkinson, Grendelkhan, Gronky, Hillthekhore, Jftuga, Kgaughan, Kl4m, M1ss1ontomars2k4, Mindmatrix, Nick, Sheep2000, Snori, Thumperward, Yarq, Ysangkok, 47 anonymous edits

DragonFly_BSD Source: http://en.wikipedia.org/w/index.php?title=DragonFly_BSD Contributors: Akanemoto, AlistairMcMillan, AnonMoos, Arjayay, Arved, AvicAWB, Ben.c.roberts, Bitmappity, Brianski, Btornado, CanisRufus, Corti, Cyan, Czarkoff, DagErlingSmørgrav, David Gerard, Delirium, Derbeth, Dittaeva, Dodell, Dysprosia, Ebasconp, Ebasco, Edward, Epolk, Epswindell, Ernstdehaan, FatalError, Feezo, Frap, Freedomlinux, Fryed-peach, Gavinatkinson, Gerbrant, Ghen, Ghettoblaster, GoldKanga, GreenReaper, Greenrd, Gsf, Gsp, Guy Harris, Gwip, Haidut, Happyrabbit, Iain.mcclatchie, Iamfscked, Icedog, Implements, Isilanes, JYolkowski, Janizary, Jerryobject, Jimfbleak, Jonkerz, KAMiKAZOW, Kathleen.wright5, Kinema, Kl4m-AWB, Lazarus, Letdorf, Lowellian, Ludootje, MJA, Markcollinsx, Markdask, Marko75, Martarius, Marudubshinki, MathewTownsend, Meangrape, Mike92591, Mindmatrix, Monoecus, Mordomo, MureninC, Neilc, Nikai, Parsreason, Pgan002, Piet Delport, Przepla, Qwitchibo, R'n'B, R. S. Shaw, RenamedUser2, Rich Farmbrough, Rjwilmsi, Ronz, Ryan Norton, SF007, Schewek, ShelfSkewed, Shooke, SilverFox, Stewartadcock, Synthetik, TakuyaMurata, Tdxofo, Tedickey, Temoto, Thattommyhall, Timofonic, Tony Sidaway, Trasz, Una Smith, Wesley crossman, William Graham, Williamanthony, Wmahan, Yworo, ZeroJanvier, Zoicon5, Ævar Arnfjörð Bjarmason, 309 anonymous edits

GNU_Lesser_General_Public_License Source: http://en.wikipedia.org/w/index.php?title=GNU_Lesser_General_Public_License Contributors: AVRS, Ahunt, Alpha 4615, Andre Engels, Anthony, Apotheon, Argento, Beland, Betterworld, Blanchardb, Bogdangiusca, Chealer, Conversion script, CrawlerMonkey, David Gerard, Dicklyon, Diptanshu.D, DirkvdM, Djmckee1, Dmitrij.ledkov, Doright, Edward, Eloquence, Enkrates, Evice, Face, Fanatix, Favonian, Fox2030, Frappucino, Furrykef, Gilgamesh, GlenPeterson, Goosey, Graue, Gronky, Hairy Dude, Hayabusa future, Hervegirod, Ibbn, InverseHypercube, Janizary, Javierito92, Jerryobject, JoeSmack, Joel Saks, Kate, Kelly Martin, Kl4m, Kl4m-AWB, Krischik, Ktdreyer, Lambda-mon key, LiDaobing, Lupin, MCMLXXXVII, Malcolmxl5, Manu.m, Markvs, MattGiuca, Matusz, Maximaximax, Merphant, Mfhall, Minghong, Mms, Nikhil500, Novalis, Palosirkka, Paranomia, Pokemonblackds, Quartz25, Raph, Rapsar, Rfl, Rfontana, Rich Farmbrough, RossPatterson, Rotem Dan, SF007, SamJohnston, Sanxiyn, Sdfisher, Shirudo, Shnout, Singhalawap, Skybon, Skyfaller, Sligocki, SnowFire, Starnestommy, Stevenj, SuperDude115, Suruena, Technion, Tedickey, Thumperward, Tim Retout, Tomb9510, Toussaint, Tregoweth, Twilsonb, Twinxor, Ultimus, Unkx80, Utcursch, Verdy p, Vvijayk, Woxxy, Wwmbes, X-Fi6, Zondor, Ævar Arnfjörð Bjarmason, 65 anonymous edits

Image Sources, Licenses and Contributors

Image:MidnightBSDLogo.svg *Source*: http://en.wikipedia.org/w/index.php?title=File:MidnightBSDLogo.svg *License*: unknown *Contributors*: User:Soursquirrel

Image:MidnightBSD.jpg *Source*: http://en.wikipedia.org/w/index.php?title=File:MidnightBSD.jpg *License*: unknown *Contributors*: Laffer1

Image:Unix history-simple.svg *Source*: http://en.wikipedia.org/w/index.php?title=File:Unix_history-simple.svg *License*: unknown *Contributors*: User:Eraserhead1, User:Infinity0, User:Sav_vas

Image:IBM360-65-1.corestore.jpg *Source*: http://en.wikipedia.org/w/index.php?title=File:IBM360-65-1.corestore.jpg *License*: unknown *Contributors*: Original uploader was ArnoldReinhold at en.wikipedia

Image:PC-DOS 1.10 screenshot.png *Source*: http://en.wikipedia.org/w/index.php?title=File:PC-DOS_1.10_screenshot.png *License*: unknown *Contributors*: Remember the dot at en.wikipedia (PNG)

Image:Apple Macintosh Desktop.png *Source*: http://en.wikipedia.org/w/index.php?title=File:Apple_Macintosh_Desktop.png *License*: unknown *Contributors*: A104375, Akhilsnair, AlistairMcMillan, BorgQueen, Chmod007, Ctachme, Diego Moya, EdC, Ferrenrock, Grm wnr, HereToHelp, N. Harmonik, Ricardo Cancho Niemietz, 4 anonymous edits

File:Unix history-simple.png *Source*: http://en.wikipedia.org/w/index.php?title=File:Unix_history-simple.png *License*: unknown *Contributors*: User:Eraserhead1

Image:First Web Server.jpg *Source*: http://en.wikipedia.org/w/index.php?title=File:First_Web_Server.jpg *License*: unknown *Contributors*: User:Coolcaesar at en.wikipedia

File:Mac OSX Lion screen.png *Source*: http://en.wikipedia.org/w/index.php?title=File:Mac_OSX_Lion_screen.png *License*: unknown *Contributors*: User:JohnHWiki

File:Ubuntu 11.10 Final.png *Source*: http://en.wikipedia.org/w/index.php?title=File:Ubuntu_11.10_Final.png *License*: unknown *Contributors*: Hydriz, KAMiKAZOW, Michael Barera, 1 anonymous edits

File:Android 4.0.png *Source*: http://en.wikipedia.org/w/index.php?title=File:Android_4.0.png *License*: unknown *Contributors*: Android Open Source project

File:Windows To Go USB Drive.png *Source*: http://en.wikipedia.org/w/index.php?title=File:Windows_To_Go_USB_Drive.png *License*: unknown *Contributors*: Adrignola, SF007, 2 anonymous edits

File:Windows 7.png *Source*: http://en.wikipedia.org/w/index.php?title=File:Windows_7.png *License*: unknown *Contributors*: Addihockey10, Althepal, AnOddName, Anakin101, Andyso, Anomie, AussieLegend, Bkell, Captaincollect1970, Crazlunatic, Drilnoth, Feinoha, FleetCommand, GSK, Grayshi, Jan Hofmann, JetBlast, Jjupiter100, Josh the Nerd, Koman90, LOL, LobStoR, Mephiles602, Ngyikp, Nicholas Love, OriginalGamer, PhilKnight, RegularBreaker, Roscelese, S0aasdf2sf, SF007, SchuminWeb, Sdrtirs, Seaphoto, Sonicdude558, Sotcr, SpaceFlight89, The 888th Avatar, Warren, Wtshymanski, 35 anonymous edits

Image:Kernel Layout.svg *Source*: http://en.wikipedia.org/w/index.php?title=File:Kernel_Layout.svg *License*: unknown *Contributors*: User:Bobbo

Image:Priv rings.svg *Source*: http://en.wikipedia.org/w/index.php?title=File:Priv_rings.svg *License*: unknown *Contributors*: Hertzsprung, 6 anonymous edits

File:Virtual memory.svg *Source*: http://en.wikipedia.org/w/index.php?title=File:Virtual_memory.svg *License*: unknown *Contributors*: User:Ehamberg

File:Dolphin FileManager.png *Source*: http://en.wikipedia.org/w/index.php?title=File:Dolphin_FileManager.png *License*: unknown *Contributors*: KDE

File:Command line.png *Source*: http://en.wikipedia.org/w/index.php?title=File:Command_line.png *License*: unknown *Contributors*: The GNU Dev team, and the Arch Linux Dev team (for the Pacman command in the example)

File:KDE 4.png *Source*: http://en.wikipedia.org/w/index.php?title=File:KDE_4.png *License*: unknown *Contributors*: KDE

File:Freebsd logo.svg *Source*: http://en.wikipedia.org/w/index.php?title=File:Freebsd_logo.svg *License*: unknown *Contributors*: Sav vas, Tael

File:FreeBSD.png *Source*: http://en.wikipedia.org/w/index.php?title=File:FreeBSD.png *License*: unknown *Contributors*: Victor

File:FreeBSD Applications.png *Source*: http://en.wikipedia.org/w/index.php?title=File:FreeBSD_Applications.png *License*: unknown *Contributors*: Jlenthe

File:Bsd daemon.jpg *Source*: http://en.wikipedia.org/w/index.php?title=File:Bsd_daemon.jpg *License*: unknown *Contributors*: Carnildo, Cuervo, Eszett, Fetchcomms, Gwen Gale, Iamunknown, Matteh, Mh, Sav vas, Stifle, Tom Morris, 3 anonymous edits

File:711-screenshot.png *Source*: http://en.wikipedia.org/w/index.php?title=File:711-screenshot.png *License*: unknown *Contributors*: Kris Moore

Image:PC-BSD logo.png *Source*: http://en.wikipedia.org/w/index.php?title=File:PC-BSD_logo.png *License*: unknown *Contributors*: Boarder8925, CyberSkull, JYolkowski, JedOs, Sfan00 IMG, Tom Morris

File:Pcbsd.png *Source*: http://en.wikipedia.org/w/index.php?title=File:Pcbsd.png *License*: unknown *Contributors*: Blackaddoer, Westeros91, Who needs names?

Image:Desktop bsd logo.png *Source*: http://en.wikipedia.org/w/index.php?title=File:Desktop_bsd_logo.png *License*: unknown *Contributors*: Calmer Waters, Carnildo, Jtalledo, LFaraone, Melesse, Shooke, Sreejithk2000

Image:Desktop bsd screenshot.png *Source*: http://en.wikipedia.org/w/index.php?title=File:Desktop_bsd_screenshot.png *License*: unknown *Contributors*: Blowdart, Dragons flight, Jtalledo, Shooke, TenPoundHammer, 1 anonymous edits

Image:GNUstepGlow.png *Source*: http://en.wikipedia.org/w/index.php?title=File:GNUstepGlow.png *License*: unknown *Contributors*: Dbenbenn, Denniss, Derbeth, Elbloggers, Imz, Rfl, Shooke, WikipediaMaster

Image:Gnustep.png *Source*: http://en.wikipedia.org/w/index.php?title=File:Gnustep.png *License*: unknown *Contributors*: User:Gürkan Sengün

File:DragonFly BSD Logo.png *Source*: http://en.wikipedia.org/w/index.php?title=File:DragonFly_BSD_Logo.png *License*: unknown *Contributors*: Joe Angrisano

File:DragonFly BSD 2.10.1 boot loader screenshot.png *Source*: http://en.wikipedia.org/w/index.php?title=File:DragonFly_BSD_2.10.1_boot_loader_screenshot.png *License*: unknown *Contributors*: The DragonFly Project

File:GNU Lesser General Public License 3 Logo.svg *Source*: http://en.wikipedia.org/w/index.php?title=File:GNU_Lesser_General_Public_License_3_Logo.svg *License*: unknown *Contributors*: User:SamJohnston

GNU Free Documentation License Version 1.2, November 2002 Copyright (C) 2000,2001,2002 Free Software Foundation, Inc. 59 Temple Place, Suite 330, Boston, MA 02111-1307 USA Everyone is permitted to copy and distribute verbatim copies of this license document, but changing it is not allowed.

0. PREAMBLE
The purpose of this License is to make a manual, textbook, or other functional and useful document "free" in the sense of freedom: to assure everyone the effective freedom to copy and redistribute it, with or without modifying it, either commercially or noncommercially. Secondarily, this License preserves for the author and publisher a way to get credit for their work, while not being considered responsible for modifications made by others. This License is a kind of "copyleft", which means that derivative works of the document must themselves be free in the same sense. It complements the GNU General Public License, which is a copyleft license designed for free software. We have designed this License in order to use it for manuals for free software, because free software needs free documentation: a free program should come with manuals providing the same freedoms that the software does. But this License is not limited to software manuals; it can be used for any textual work, regardless of subject matter or whether it is published as a printed book. We recommend this License principally for works whose purpose is instruction or reference.
1. APPLICABILITY AND DEFINITIONS
This License applies to any manual or other work, in any medium, that contains a notice placed by the copyright holder saying it can be distributed under the terms of this License. Such a notice grants a world-wide, royalty-free license, unlimited in duration, to use that work under the conditions stated herein. The "Document", below, refers to any such manual or work. Any member of the public is a licensee, and is addressed as "you". You accept the license if you copy, modify or distribute the work in a way requiring permission under copyright law. A "Modified Version" of the Document means any work containing the Document or a portion of it, either copied verbatim, or with modifications and/or translated into another language. A "Secondary Section" is a named appendix or a front-matter section of the Document that deals exclusively with the relationship of the publishers or authors of the Document to the Document's overall subject (or to related matters) and contains nothing that could fall directly within that overall subject. (Thus, if the Document is in part a textbook of mathematics, a Secondary Section may not explain any mathematics.) The relationship could be a matter of historical connection with the subject or with related matters, or of legal, commercial, philosophical, ethical or political position regarding them. The "Invariant Sections" are certain Secondary Sections whose titles are designated, as being those of Invariant Sections, in the notice that says that the Document is released under this License. If a section does not fit the above definition of Secondary then it is not allowed to be designated as Invariant. The Document may contain zero Invariant Sections. If the Document does not identify any Invariant Sections then there are none. The "Cover Texts" are certain short passages of text that are listed, as Front-Cover Texts or Back-Cover Texts, in the notice that says that the Document is released under this License. A Front-Cover Text may be at most 5 words, and a Back-Cover Text may be at most 25 words. A "Transparent" copy of the Document means a machine-readable copy, represented in a format whose specification is available to the general public, that is suitable for revising the document straightforwardly with generic text editors or (for images composed of pixels) generic paint programs or (for drawings) some widely available drawing editor, and that is suitable for input to text formatters or for automatic translation to a variety of formats suitable for input to text formatters. A copy made in an otherwise Transparent file format whose markup, or absence of markup, has been arranged to thwart or discourage subsequent modification by readers is not Transparent. An image format is not Transparent if used for any substantial amount of text. A copy that is not "Transparent" is called "Opaque". Examples of suitable formats for Transparent copies include plain ASCII without markup, Texinfo input format, LaTeX input format, SGML or XML using a publicly available DTD, and standard-conforming simple HTML, PostScript or PDF designed for human modification. Examples of transparent image formats include PNG, XCF and JPG. Opaque formats include proprietary formats that can be read and edited only by proprietary word processors, SGML or XML for which the DTD and/or processing tools are not generally available, and the machine-generated HTML, PostScript or PDF produced by some word processors for output purposes only. The "Title Page" means, for a printed book, the title page itself, plus such following pages as are needed to hold, legibly, the material this License requires to appear in the title page. For works in formats which do not have any title page as such, "Title Page" means the text near the most prominent appearance of the work's title, preceding the beginning of the body of the text. A section "Entitled XYZ" means a named subunit of the Document whose title either is precisely XYZ or contains XYZ in parentheses following text that translates XYZ in another language. (Here XYZ stands for a specific section name mentioned below, such as "Acknowledgements", "Dedications", "Endorsements", or "History".) To "Preserve the Title" of such a section when you modify the Document means that it remains a section "Entitled XYZ" according to this definition. The Document may include Warranty Disclaimers next to the notice which states that this License applies to the Document. These Warranty Disclaimers are considered to be included by reference in this License, but only as regards disclaiming warranties: any other implication that these Warranty Disclaimers may have is void and has no effect on the meaning of this License.
2. VERBATIM COPYING
You may copy and distribute the Document in any medium, either commercially or noncommercially, provided that this License, the copyright notices, and the license notice saying this License applies to the Document are reproduced in all copies, and that you add no other conditions whatsoever to those of this License. You may not use technical measures to obstruct or control the reading or further copying of the copies you make or distribute. However, you may accept compensation in exchange for copies. If you distribute a large enough number of copies you must also follow the conditions in section 3. You may also lend copies, under the same conditions stated above, and you may publicly display copies.
3. COPYING IN QUANTITY
If you publish printed copies (or copies in media that commonly have printed covers) of the Document, numbering more than 100, and the Document's license notice requires Cover Texts, you must enclose the copies in covers that carry, clearly and legibly, all these Cover Texts: Front-Cover Texts on the front cover, and Back-Cover Texts on the back cover. Both covers must also clearly and legibly identify you as the publisher of these copies. The front cover must present the full title with all words of the title equally prominent and visible. You may add other material on the covers in addition. Copying with changes limited to the covers, as long as they preserve the title of the Document and satisfy these conditions, can be treated as verbatim copying in other respects. If the required texts for either cover are too voluminous to fit legibly, you should put the first ones listed (as many as fit reasonably) on the actual cover, and continue the rest onto adjacent pages. If you publish or distribute Opaque copies of the Document numbering more than 100, you must either include a machine-readable Transparent copy along with each Opaque copy, or state in or with each Opaque copy a computer-network location from which the general network-using public has access to download using public-standard network protocols a complete Transparent copy of the Document, free of added material. If you use the latter option, you must take reasonably prudent steps, when you begin distribution of Opaque copies in quantity, to ensure that this Transparent copy will remain thus accessible at the stated location until at least one year after the last time you distribute an Opaque copy (directly or through your agents or retailers) of that edition to the public. It is requested, but not required, that you contact the authors of the Document well before redistributing any large number of copies, to give them a chance to provide you with an updated version of the Document.
4. MODIFICATIONS
You may copy and distribute a Modified Version of the Document under the conditions of sections 2 and 3 above, provided that you release the Modified Version under precisely this License, with the Modified Version filling the role of the Document, thus licensing distribution and modification of the Modified Version to whoever possesses a copy of it. In addition, you must do these things in the Modified Version: A. Use in the Title Page (and on the covers, if any) a title distinct from that of the Document, and from those of previous versions (which should, if there were any, be listed in the History section of the Document). You may use the same title as a previous version if the original publisher of that version gives permission. B. List on the Title Page, as authors, one or more persons or entities responsible for authorship of the modifications in the Modified Version, together with at least five of the principal authors of the Document (all of its principal authors, if it has fewer than five), unless they release you from this requirement. C. State on the Title page the name of the publisher of the Modified Version, as the publisher. D. Preserve all the copyright notices of the Document. E. Add an appropriate copyright notice for your modifications adjacent to the other copyright notices. F. Include, immediately after the copyright notices, a license notice giving the public permission to use the Modified Version under the terms of this License, in the form shown in the Addendum below. G. Preserve in that license notice the full lists of Invariant Sections and required Cover Texts given in the Document's license notice. H. Include an unaltered copy of this License. I. Preserve the section Entitled "History", Preserve its Title, and add to it an item stating at least the title, year, new authors, and publisher of the Modified Version as given on the Title Page. If there is no section Entitled "History" in the Document, create one stating the title, year, authors, and publisher of the Document as given on its Title Page, then add an item describing the Modified Version as stated in the previous sentence. J. Preserve the network location, if any, given in the Document for public access to a Transparent copy of the Document, and likewise the network locations given in the Document for previous versions it was based on. These may be placed in the "History" section. You may omit a network location for a work that was published at least four years before the Document itself, or if the original publisher of the version it refers to gives permission. K. For any section Entitled "Acknowledgements" or "Dedications", Preserve the Title of the section, and preserve in the section all the substance and tone of each of the contributor acknowledgements and/or dedications given therein. L. Preserve all the Invariant Sections of the Document, unaltered in their text and in their titles. Section numbers or the equivalent are not considered part of the section titles. M. Delete any section Entitled "Endorsements". Such a section may not be included in the Modified Version. N. Do not retitle any existing section to be Entitled "Endorsements" or to conflict in title with any Invariant Section. O. Preserve any Warranty Disclaimers. If the Modified Version includes new front-matter sections or appendices that qualify as Secondary Sections and contain no material copied from the Document, you may at your option designate some or all of these sections as invariant. To do this, add their titles to the list of Invariant Sections in the Modified Version's license notice. These titles must be distinct from any other section titles. You may add a section Entitled "Endorsements", provided it contains nothing but endorsements of your Modified Version by various parties--for example, statements of peer review or that the text has been approved by an organization as the authoritative definition of a standard. You may add a passage of up to five words as a Front-Cover Text, and a passage of up to 25 words as a Back-Cover Text, to the end of the list of Cover Texts in the Modified Version. Only one passage of Front-Cover Text and one of Back-Cover Text may be added by (or through arrangements made by) any one entity. If the Document already includes a cover text for the same cover, previously added by you or by arrangement made by the same entity you are acting on behalf of, you may not add another; but you may replace the old one, on explicit permission from the previous publisher that added the old one. The author(s) and publisher(s) of the Document do not by this License give permission to use their names for publicity for or to assert or imply endorsement of any Modified Version.
5. COMBINING DOCUMENTS
You may combine the Document with other documents released under this License, under the terms defined in section 4 above for modified versions, provided that you include in the combination all of the Invariant Sections of all of the original documents, unmodified, and list them all as Invariant Sections of your combined work in its license notice, and that you preserve all their Warranty Disclaimers. The combined work need only contain one copy of this License, and multiple identical Invariant Sections may be replaced with a single copy. If there are multiple Invariant Sections with the same name but different contents, make the title of each such section unique by adding at the end of it, in parentheses, the name of the original author or publisher of that section if known, or else a unique number. Make the same adjustment to the section titles in the list of Invariant Sections in the license notice of the combined work. In the combination, you must combine any sections Entitled "History" in the various original documents, forming one section Entitled "History"; likewise combine any sections Entitled "Acknowledgements", and any sections Entitled "Dedications". You must delete all sections Entitled "Endorsements".
6. COLLECTIONS OF DOCUMENTS
You may make a collection consisting of the Document and other documents released under this License, and replace the individual copies of this License in the various documents with a single copy that is included in the collection, provided that you follow the rules of this License for verbatim copying of each of the documents in all other respects. You may extract a single document from such a collection, and distribute it individually under this License, provided you insert a copy of this License into the extracted document, and follow this License in all other respects regarding verbatim copying of that document.
7. AGGREGATION WITH INDEPENDENT WORKS
A compilation of the Document or its derivatives with other separate and independent documents or works, in or on a volume of a storage or distribution medium, is called an "aggregate" if the copyright resulting from the compilation is not used to limit the legal rights of the compilation's users beyond what the individual works permit. When the Document is included in an aggregate, this License does not apply to the other works in the aggregate which are not themselves derivative works of the Document. If the Cover Text requirement of section 3 is applicable to these copies of the Document, then if the Document is less than one half of the entire aggregate, the Document's Cover Texts may be placed on covers that bracket the Document within the aggregate, or the electronic equivalent of covers if the Document is in electronic form. Otherwise they must appear on printed covers that bracket the whole aggregate.
8. TRANSLATION
Translation is considered a kind of modification, so you may distribute translations of the Document under the terms of section 4. Replacing Invariant Sections with translations requires special permission from their copyright holders, but you may include translations of some or all Invariant Sections in addition to the original versions of these Invariant Sections. You may include a translation of this License, and all the license notices in the Document, and any Warranty Disclaimers, provided that you also include the original English version of this License and the original versions of those notices and disclaimers. In case of a disagreement between the translation and the original version of this License or a notice or disclaimer, the original version will prevail. If a section in the Document is Entitled "Acknowledgements", "Dedications", or "History", the requirement (section 4) to Preserve its Title (section 1) will typically require changing the actual title.
9. TERMINATION
You may not copy, modify, sublicense, or distribute the Document except as expressly provided for under this License. Any other attempt to copy, modify, sublicense or distribute the Document is void, and will automatically terminate your rights under this License. However, parties who have received copies, or rights, from you under this License will not have their licenses terminated so long as such parties remain in full compliance.
10. FUTURE REVISIONS OF THIS LICENSE
The Free Software Foundation may publish new, revised versions of the GNU Free Documentation License from time to time. Such new versions will be similar in spirit to the present version, but may differ in detail to address new problems or concerns. See http://www.gnu.org/copyleft/. Each version of the License is given a distinguishing version number. If the Document specifies that a particular numbered version of this License "or any later version" applies to it, you have the option of following the terms and conditions either of that specified version or of any later version that has been published (not as a draft) by the Free Software Foundation. If the Document does not specify a version number of this License, you may choose any version ever published (not as a draft) by the Free Software Foundation. ADDENDUM: How to use this License for your documents To use this License in a document you have written, include a copy of the License in the document and put the following copyright and license notices just after the title page: Copyright (c) YEAR YOUR NAME. Permission is granted to copy, distribute and/or modify this document under the terms of the GNU Free Documentation License, Version 1.2 or any later version published by the Free Software Foundation; with no Invariant Sections, no Front-Cover Texts, and no Back-Cover Texts. A copy of the license is included in the section entitled "GNU Free Documentation License". If you have Invariant Sections, Front-Cover Texts and Back-Cover Texts, replace the "with...Texts." line with this: with the Invariant Sections being LIST THEIR TITLES, with the Front-Cover Texts being LIST, and with the Back-Cover Texts being LIST. If you have Invariant Sections without Cover Texts, or some other combination of the three, merge those two alternatives to suit the situation. If your document contains nontrivial examples of program code, we recommend releasing these examples in parallel under your choice of free software license, such as the GNU General Public License, to permit their use in free software.

Printed by Books on Demand GmbH, Norderstedt / Germany